PRAISE FOR THIS BOOK

The Dance of Love is a soulful relationship playbook you'll return to for years to come. If you crave synergy between the masculine and feminine energies in your relationships—romantic or otherwise—and you're willing to embrace ownership of your role in co-creating love, Ann offers profound perspective shifts, embodied insights, and practical tools to help you become a skilled cultivator of connection, intimacy, and fulfillment. Even if you've never stepped on the Aikido mat, you'll feel its wisdom flow through your relationships.

—Kyle Jason Leitzke, *Life Fulfillment Coach,*
Men's Mentor, Aikido Practitioner, and Founder of
The Fulfillment Code™ & Sacred Brotherhood

In her latest book, *The Dance of Love,* Ann O'Brien seamlessly blends her wealth of experience as an Intuitive Healer, Personal Development Coach and Black Belt Sensei. She draws insightful parallels between the physical, on-the-mat practice of Aikido and the internal dynamics of relating to ourselves and others. Opportunities for growth and reflection are offered throughout in the form of practical worksheets that walk us through self-discovery in a step by step fashion. This blending of sensitive inquiry supported by a strong framework of practical guidance is what makes the book uniquely useful.

The Dance of Love reads easily and is approachable by all those seeking balance, connection and joyfulness in their lives, whether martial artists or not.

—Melissa Pittman Fischer,
Godan (5th degree Black Belt), Tenzan Aikido Seattle

Through the fundamentals of Aikido, personal stories and well positioned analogies of life on and off the mat, Ann beautifully weaves the practice of Aikido into managing the myriads of complexities that make up the reality of our personal relationships. She has succeeded in creating a guidebook for those who are looking to create healthier relationships with both others and the self all while approaching life from a more centered and grounded place. This book truly is intended to guide the reader through the concept of "living life as a martial art."

—**Erik "Yoda" DaRosa,** *founder of U-MOST Retreats and the "From Survivor to Thriver" podcast*

The Dance of Love is a beautiful and powerful approach to relationship dynamics. It covers a very complicated subject—learning how to do life in partnership with others while understanding and rediscovering ourselves—in a fun way that's easy to grasp. Can›t recommend it enough.

—**Cristina Costanzo,** *Aikido Yondan (4th degree black belt) and Relational Wisdom Coach (AikiSkills and Human-Game)*

Ann O'Brien was one of my first teachers in intuitive development, energy healing, and psychic protection beginning in 2012, and her work has continued to ripple through my life ever since. It's been an honor to voice her audiobooks, and *The Dance of Love* has quickly become one of my favorites. Ann beautifully blends Aikido wisdom with spiritual insight to show how receiving and responding—far from being passive or reactive—are sacred, embodied practices that create real connection. This book offers a powerful reframe of relationship as a dynamic, living art form—one that honors both sensitivity and strength. It's not just a guide—it's a transmission for anyone ready to walk the path of love with intention, presence, and soul.

—**Elysia Skye,** *Intuitive Guide & Creator of The Brilliance Method Podcast & Coaching Program®*

the DANCE OF LOVE

Mastering Your Relationships through Aikido Wisdom

ANN O'BRIEN

Publisher's Note

This book is intended to support you in your personal relationships and self-healing path. That said, the techniques, exercises and suggestions offered in this book are not promised or intended to take the place of psychological or other professional services. When expert assistance is needed, one should enlist the help of a qualified professional.

Bible quotation is from the Berean Standard Bible, accessed through www.biblehub.com.

Book cover design by Lucinda Raye.

Name: Ann O'Brien, author.

Title: *The Dance of Love: Mastering Your Relationships through Aikido Wisdom*

ISBN 978-1-7344128-3-3

To all who have shared kuzushi with me.
Through these Divine disruptions,
I have sprung forth in greater love.

Table of Contents

Introduction

You can argue with relationship advice, or with philosophies about men and women. You can't really argue with the laws of physics. If you feel something in your body, you're probably going to believe it. This is a book that attempts to convey the full body knowing of dynamic love that I have discovered in my Aikido practice.

Aikido is a martial art that brings us to unity. This is neither the merging of co-dependence nor the neutralization of roles that is currently trendy. In its dance of feminine and masculine, give and receive, attack and surrender—polarity is ever-present. We learn to live in a continual state of aliveness. Through the play within technique, we learn to participate in love as if our lives depend on it. They do.

If you've ever been sick after a breakup or disagreement with a loved one, if you've felt the flatness of not knowing your purpose or feeling excited about anything—you know well the weight of trying to live without love. If you're familiar with the *blah blah blah* of perpetual disappointment, if you've space-walked through more days than you care to count just going through the motions—you know what it feels like when life force stops.

By contrast, the rush of energy in your body when you're in love—or living your passion—is electrifying. This fire within you has immense healing power—for both you and those around you. From this place, though you fully express your individuality, separation is something you can't even entertain.

Most people aren't familiar with Aikido, but they have many concepts about love. As an intuitive healer for more than two decades, I see people struggling with relationships more than anything. The bliss of love fulfilled can quickly switch to immense pain when it goes away or violates our expectations. So, how can we keep love going?

I wrote this book to support you in giving and receiving love fully and effectively through your body and life, according to Aikido principles. You can certainly use the philosophies in this book in your love life. Yet your *partner* at any moment may be a co-worker, a family member, an aspect of your life, or even a condition in the world that bugs you. When you are switched on and living this dance each moment, you feel the bliss of life force and you co-create the truth of love everywhere you go.

As we each resolve our personal relationships and learn to live in harmony with life force, I believe we contribute to healing the planet. This means we must abandon both fighting to hurt and hurting because we don't fight. We must be willing to fight in order to love more. As we do this as individuals, I sense we won't need the shadow reflection of war—both physical and otherwise. When we feel the fullness of love's expression, I believe we will be healthier and wealthier. These things are implicit when we choose life over death.

Onegaishimasu. Will you please practice with me?

My Story

At 19 years old, I moved from Florida to Santa Cruz, California, with my then-boyfriend in my tiny Honda CRX and "our" VW van. After the van broke down, we shared the car and a studio apartment underneath a home in the mountains, commuting into town for school and work from 7 a.m.–7 p.m. I used to go into the bathroom—the only place I could close a door—to write in my journal and get some space. He didn't like this.

I had to take a PhysEd class for college. Aikido lit up in my list of choices and I signed up. For a month or two, I attended classes that brought me into my center. I learned healthy assertiveness and how to blend, roll, and fall safely.

As the semester progressed, we were traveling so much that I wasn't keeping up with consistent classes. The "falling" part of the practice still felt clunky, and I became concerned I'd get hurt. Tears fell the day I told my boyfriend I'd decided to quit Aikido during our drive into town. "Why are you crying?" he asked me. It surprised me, too, and time would reveal the answer.

I'd touched on something I couldn't yet sustain. For the first time in my life, I'd sensed my capacity to manage all the energy I felt, and to really keep my center around other people. It was a baby step, but I knew it was something I needed.

A few years after my breakup from this entangled love, I found Aikido again. I was at a Buddhist-inspired graduate school in Boulder, Colorado. For my writing degree, I had to take an Eastern philosophy type of class, and there it was again. I signed up. More ready this time, I dove in deep with a wise and compassionate teacher. I felt like she could see right through me, and this plus the training healed me.

When the offer came to assist kids' class at the local dojo, I followed my instant "yes." That semester was the beginning of four years of training at Boulder Aikikai with Hiroshi Ikeda Sensei, a master teacher. When the kids' teacher I was assisting retired, I took over teaching the class.

I remember the guys coming in for practice as I was finishing with the kids. I sensed they were rolling their eyes, mocking our games. These men seemed so serious and rigid. "What am I doing here?" I wondered. I felt tired of the uniform, hierarchy, and regimentation. I wanted to laugh, play, and wear bright colors. Training with children was more fun than with adults.

Gradually, my evenings took me to African dance class and away from Aikido. Frustrated in my love life, I concluded that my training not only took too much time; it was too masculine. "I need to embody more feminine energy," I told myself as I put away my uniform and quit for the second time.

Now, I know it wasn't Aikido's fault. I'd grown up with a tough-guy, veteran father and a mother who obsessively watched sports. With short hair and no makeup, her feminine energy expressed as, "Aww, Jim, I don't know how to run the dishwasher. Can you turn it on for me?" I didn't want to copy that helplessness, so I focused on being smart and strong, which were qualities I got rewarded for.

Around the time I quit Aikido in Boulder, I embarked on a year-long psychic development program. Our learning was not so much about fortune-telling as much as it was about energy mastery. It gave me some of the same benefits as Aikido—I learned to ground myself, clear energy, and distinguish my truth from other people's. That year-long class led to 10 years of training, and to my professional practice as an intuitive teacher and healer.

Some years later, I got really into yoga. I studied tantric philosophy and conscious relationships. Finally, I found more softness in my body and simultaneously, my love life started to blossom. I taught yoga for a few years, then became a mother and let it go, save for a little home practice. I kept up my intuitive business, offering 1/1 sessions and classes, mostly by phone or online.

I never planned to go back to Aikido, yet there was a depth I missed and wanted. I'd graduated myself from my yoga and spiritual teachers. I felt I had gotten somewhere, and didn't need to seek outside myself so much. Still, I yearned for an anchor, a guiding light, a practice I could go deep with.

About a year before I resumed training, I knew Aikido would come back. I courted it through study, and by writing and speaking about the philosophy frequently. I searched online and traveled to explore dojos. One morning I woke with a vivid dream of a prominent female teacher. With startling clarity, she told me, "In Aikido, you unite masculine and feminine in your body." This felt like my Divine wink, the key to the door back into my practice.

I went back to Boulder to visit. Seeing one of my former teachers, who had once somewhat intimidated me, was suddenly so easy. He approached me as I walked in, and our energies blended with as much fluidity as I'd felt on the mat. I realized I had shifted. Now, our connection felt more available, more open than ever. I didn't even get on the mat; it was just a simple hello, but it had impact.

In 2017 I returned to Aikido, and joined a new dojo in Carbondale, Colorado. Shortly after joining, I was invited to teach kids' classes there, and I did so for three years.

As for my own training, I was blessed to have a highly

skilled teacher who focused on *ukemi*, the art of receiving technique. As he was just getting established in our little mountain town, many of my classes turned into private lessons. There had been Aikido in the area before, and so a large percentage of those who did attend were black belts.

Immersed in this high-level training, I deepened my capacity to respond accurately. I honed both my understanding that receiving is a choice—as well as my skills in how to do so. On the mat, this translated into safe and dynamic practice. In my intuitive work, it supported my philosophy that sensitivity is strength, provided you know how to work with it. In my personal relationships and relationship coaching, I began to receive more, and to offer true feminine power.

In 2021 that dojo closed, and I resumed teaching and training in 2022. I pray not only to carry forth the Aikido lineage, but also to be a part of the evolution of Divine love on Earth. I wish to share this with you here.

Aikido, the Way of Harmonizing Life Force

Aikido is a modern Japanese martial art founded by Morihei Ueshiba, otherwise known as O Sensei. The word *Aikido* is made up of three *kanji*, or characters in Japanese. *Ai* means harmony or unifying. *Ki* translates to energy or spirit. And *do* equates to the way or path. Altogether, Aikido is the way of harmonizing with life force energy.

Aikido is a defensive martial art in that we focus on redirecting our opponent's energy rather than sparring or fighting. In fact, we refer to the other person as our *partner*, with the goal being to protect *both* ourselves and them.

While some schools and practitioners today take a softer, more energetic approach, other Aikido styles are highly martial. The attacker employs various grabs and strikes, from which we can execute various throws, joint manipulations, and pins. Much of the practice is the art of receiving these techniques gracefully and safely. As we do, conflict ceases, and *peace* may look like one person flipping and tumbling in exhilaration.

Besides open hand training, we also practice with a wooden sword (*bokken*), staff (*jo*), and knife (*tanto*). Weapons work teaches precision and appropriate distance as it heightens martial awareness. Because Aikido has roots in swordsmanship, many elements of weapons practice translate directly to open hand technique.

Respect, etiquette, and tradition are important at the Aikido dojo. We bow when we enter or leave the room or mat, as well as when we start and end class. Within class, we bow to our partners before and after practicing each technique. We say "onegaishimasu" and "Domo arigato gozaimashita" (fancy ways of saying "please" and "thank you") when we bow in and out. And it's expected that we show honor to our senior students and teachers as well as support those newer to training. There are many other customs pertaining to Aikido uniform, how we practice, and more. You will find nuances in etiquette if you visit different dojos.

Some Westerners love this ritual, and many find it takes getting used to. Aikido is not a religion, and the rules are not designed to strip us of our power—far from it. The emphasis is on respect, and ultimately when you respect another you are respecting yourself. As we give thanks to those who paved the way for our practice, we tap into their wisdom and then emanate it. When we advance, we take on more responsibility, not less. Ideally, this minimizes ego gratification and the likelihood of putting those in power on a pedestal. Of course, humans still do it, but Aikido seeks to polish us.

Polarity Is Essential to Unity

Aikido is sometimes called the art of peace. The paradox here is that it *is* a martial art. If there's no conflict, there's nothing to unify and it's all fluff. The violent, martial aspect is what makes peace so meaningful. It's not that we seek to hurt someone, but we need to know where the art has the potential to cause harm. When we do, we train with full aliveness—always remembering that possibility. One of my *senpai* (a student senior to me) shared how completely exposed he felt being thrown by high-level teachers. Training "on the edge" like this led him to surrender more fully.

The feminine is the part of us that responds and receives. If no one does this, we butt heads and love can't flow. The masculine is the part of us which witnesses and directs energy. If no one does this, there is just mush—no edge, no clarity, a pretty dance at best.

Healthy versus Unhealthy Feminine

If only feminine energy was always expressed in a beautiful way—it would be easier to both embody and respect. Unfortunately, most of us have had countless experiences of its less-helpful side. This is not about pointing fingers. At some point, each of us has likely acted as the toxic feminine. This can happen if the healthy feminine was not modeled to us, or if we haven't learned any better ways to get our needs met.

In order to realize unity, I feel we need to find and embrace the healthy feminine. As clarity comes through contrast, it may help to define what this is *not*. Here are some of the many reasons I've seen folks mistrust the feminine:

"I don't want to be like my mom … she was so disempowered."

"I don't want anything to do with those catty, gossipy girls I grew up with."

"Women can be so fake and manipulative. I just want to be myself."

"I'm tired of guilt trips. I'm tired of her expecting me to read her mind."

"She's nuts. Her emotions are out of control."

"She never stops talking. She nitpicks every little thing."

All of these are complaints about the *toxic* feminine. Yet, to discard all feminine energy because of these types of bad experiences would be a grave misunderstanding.

Throughout history, the feminine *has* often shown up as passive, manipulative, disempowered, needy, indirect, hyper-emotional, controlling, or phony. Since these energies don't feel good, many conscious people have gone on to reject feminine energy entirely.

Even those of us who understand and *want* to be in our

healthy feminine may hesitate to do it. Because the feminine energy is inherently receptive, we can be quite prickly or guarded if we've previously felt unsafe in receiving. We may have had negative experiences—ranging from severe to mild abuse, to being put down, to not knowing how to manage ourselves in relation to all that we feel. If so, it may be tempting to shut down or put up walls.

The feminine is naturally wildly creative and expressive. I liken it to a river, with the healthy masculine being the riverbank. But if you haven't had any good riverbanks in your life or have been told (out loud or not) to tone it down, this part of you will also feel unsafe to express.

It amuses me that "feminism" is rarely approached in a feminine way. It tends not to be pro-feminine, because it doesn't celebrate healthy feminine energy. Instead, it asserts how women are strong like men. And so, it's enforcing the very thing it says it's against (that masculine energy is superior).

So, what is healthy feminine? It's receptive, responsive, creative, nurturing, and focused on love and connection. These parts of ourselves get better and better the more we embrace them. For example, instead of getting overwhelmed by everything I feel, I can recognize my feeling nature and choose how to care for it. Rather than becoming a dumping ground for other people's stress, I can respond based on what does and doesn't feel good to me.

Receiving is not passive. In both Aikido and conscious love, it is active, highly expressive, and fully chosen. With a focus on cultivating love and nurturing life, we are less likely to destroy or compete.

Relating with the healthy masculine—within ourselves, our lives, or our Aikido practice—brings out the best in our feminine. And so, we'll cover what that is next.

Healthy versus Unhealthy Masculine

When masculine energy shows up in a greedy, domineering way—our distaste for it makes sense. Because men have stronger muscles and social positioning, the uproar over men's abuse of power can be equally big. Whether the masculine has more power to hurt is up for debate; however, it may seem so from a material viewpoint. And here, we are having a cultural moment where justice is being called for.

I am saddened though, when the healthy masculine gets trampled by this uproar. Without the true masculine in each of us and our society, we also suffer. When it comes from service and with compassion, masculine energy is tremendously healing.

What does this look like? In keeping with the river and riverbank analogy, the healthy masculine both holds the feminine and supports her expression. She shapes him and he directs her. These things happen naturally. Neither the river nor the riverbank is heavy-handed or contriving in this dynamic.

The gifts of the masculine include structure, direction, protecting, providing, penetrating, and driving things beyond prior limits. We will discuss these qualities throughout this book, as they show up in our Aikido practice and relationships. Each of these gifts are enlivening, and they are needed.

Just as the masculine can be domineering and greedy, so can the feminine. It just looks different. I would argue that the problem is in whether one is coming from "taking" versus "giving," and not within either masculine or feminine energy alone.

One can nurture out of desire for her own gain, and/or

one can love unconditionally. Another may direct and guide to boost his ego, or he could teach and inspire from a place of pure service. The difference is noticeable, and we all tend to recoil in the face of selfishness, even if it's dressed up as something else.

I would love to see more of us spot the root imbalances here, and to quit jumping to blame men or blame women. Just as the healthy masculine can heal the feminine, the healthy feminine inspires the masculine to show up better. It is a disservice to all of us when we say, "It's not my problem to help my partner." Each of us has the responsibility to bring our best selves if we want those around us to change, and doing this should not be a burden.

I truly believe we must celebrate the healthy masculine and feminine when we see them, for their expression is key to a thriving life. Beyond positioning us to enjoy sacred love with another human, honoring each of these aspects will allow us to stay close to our own life force in an increasingly numb and disconnected world.

The Roles We Play

At any given moment, each of us may embody either masculine or feminine energy. We all have both sides, though one or the other may be dominant some or all of the time. By becoming more conscious about the energy we're expressing in any given moment, we live as more empowered, whole, and vital human beings. In addition, our relationships become more dynamic and life-affirming.

In Aikido practice, there are two primary roles: 1) *Uke* – the attacker, who then typically gets thrown and 2) *Nage* – the one who is attacked, and then applies technique to control the uke. Each must play both the feminine and masculine roles, yet just one role at a time. When the roles get muddy, Aikido stops.

For example, the uke must strike with full commitment, offering masculine energy. She then quickly becomes the receiver, embodying feminine energy as her partner redirects her strike. At this point, she must flow and respond to nage's movement in order to protect herself.

Nage, the one who executes the throw or pin, initially takes the feminine role by demonstrating openness and invitation. He quickly becomes the masculine partner as he is attacked, at which time he must clearly drive the interaction, taking care of himself as well as his partner.

Imagine if both parties tried to direct the encounter at the same time. That would be a fight. Someone might get hurt, or the energy could just get stuck. I've come home from enough classes with bruised arms to know!

While many of us have been conditioned to *go-go-go*, always driving in life, it gets old when we never downshift. This is how physical tension builds up in our bodies. This is when people talk over each other, or when they listen to respond but not to understand. Operating from here, we may feel we need to perform or be perfect, or that we're responsible for everything all the time. When two people like this get together, they may have a business relationship at best. Otherwise, there is little interaction to be had.

What if both partners primarily live in the flow? For instance, one says, "What do you want to do tomorrow?"

And the other replies, "I don't know; whatever you want to do." This could go on and on as they pass a joint between them and watch the sunset. Beauty turns quickly into boredom. Peace flattens into numbness, and nothing gets done.

Since masculine qualities have been rewarded in recent history, many couples have found themselves in a business arrangement and have lost the spark. And in the workplace, empathy and cooperation tend to take second place to goals and tasks.

There have been many positive shifts in these areas recently, however I have also seen the opposite problems. Work meetings that go on for hours as everyone voices their feelings can be exhausting and unproductive. Always letting that friend or family member off the hook because you feel for them, even though their behavior is hurting you, will wear you down.

As the masculine has been criticized or even disowned, many of my feminine clients have felt frustrated. "Where are the good, strong men?" they ask. While they may appreciate a sensitive guy, they also long to feel protected, provided for, claimed, or pursued.

Cultivating the Dance of Relationship

Aikido is a continuous exchange of feminine and masculine energies, the union of which has the potential to create life. After intensive practice such as a seminar, my body feels like it's pulsing with spirals—as if my DNA gets activated. And this makes sense when we remember it is an art designed to preserve life, not to hurt or kill.

While we must find center to express the healthiest versions of whatever energy comes through us, in its full expression Aikido requires polarity. I believe any truly fulfilling relationship or life is no different.

How can we be simultaneously centered, and also embodying either masculine or feminine? In practice, this feels to me like an extremely high level of attunement. It is part of what keeps Aikido an art, beyond the realm of just "roughhousing." Even as we attack, fall, or throw, we are incredibly alert. At any given moment, this allows us to change course, amplify, or soften as needed.

Our appropriate energy expression is most evident in relationship. There's not much to receive, direct, or protect in a vacuum. We bring these things out in each other. If you push towards me, I lean back. If you lean back, I move forward.

On the mat, I'd likely meet a strongly directed attack (masculine energy) by turning and letting it pass (feminine energy) before I dealt with it. On the other hand, I could catch that same attack by redirecting it early when it was still soft, and had yet to build momentum. At this stage, an attack is more "feminine," and partner can apply masculine power to it.

The greater our mastery in both Aikido and conscious

relating, we perceive more and more subtle shifts in the energy around us. We know things before they happen. On the mat, we see the attack before the external eyes can see. In love, we can feel how our partner feels, even across the globe.

From our wounding, we can also psychically track someone and make ourselves and others crazy in the process. This behavior, rooted in anxiety and trauma, will neither make us feel better nor get us what we want. This is true no matter how accurate we are. Instead, approaching our relationships from a grounded love allows us to master our awareness so that we instead serve everyone involved.

Learning the Art of Receiving

In my early Aikido training, I sometimes felt nervous about training with those better than me. My ego would choose people at or below my level, and then get frustrated when we struggled through class. Pretty soon, I gravitated towards skilled practitioners who could either guide me or flow with me, whatever was needed in the moment.

Around that same time, I dated men who weren't ready, or who wouldn't commit. In retrospect, this was the same ego move as choosing beginners as my training partners. It seemed emotionally *safer* at the time, yet I came to see that I also had this backwards. These unavailable relationships at best went nowhere, and at worst brought a lot of pain.

To play in the dance of love, we must be able to receive. The ego doesn't know how. Despite our toxic masculine programming that says, "be tough at all costs" and the wounded feminine misunderstanding that says receiving is unsafe, we know differently deep down. This is because we are made of masculine and feminine essences; their natural expressions are implicit in our life.

Our world prioritizes masculine power over feminine receptivity. I have seen this even in the "feminist" movement, which has insisted that women can do all that men can do. While this is fine in and of itself, it has left open the question of how to be empowered in our receiving.

On the Aikido mat, over time I came to see that receiving is a choice. I realized it was good for me, the giver, and the greater world. Anyone who becomes advanced at anything must receive *a lot* in order to get there. Aikido is an art of energy transmission, and the path to more dynamic training is to *feel* it through physical practice with those at a higher level.

In daily interactions, any time one person shows up with more love and awareness—whether that means drawing closer or setting a boundary—both people benefit. Can we learn to unguard ourselves enough to allow this?

Not only does your receiving demonstrate self-respect, it also supports your partner to relate with you in more fulfilling ways. For instance, if I am really good at falling and rolling, my partner can apply Aikido technique with full force and speed.

Off the mat, my partner can bring more of himself when I am emotionally present and open. Have you ever met someone you felt totally relaxed with, and free to be your whole self? This is invigorating for all parties. And it only happens when there is receptivity. Your receptivity is not selfish; it is, in fact, deeply healing to those who have something to share.

Writing Practice:
How Is Your Relationship with Receiving?

It's one thing to say, "I should get better at receiving" and try to make yourself do it. You may succeed some of the time.

To really unravel our rigidity, we generally need to know why it's there. The most common reasons I see why people don't receive are:

- Receiving feels unsafe, due to past hurts or trauma.
- It feels overwhelming, for those highly sensitive.
- Our society prizes independence, doing, and achieving.
- We're already full, due to too much input and lack of space (physical, emotional, mental, or energetic).
- We haven't learned how. Healthy receiving wasn't modeled for us.

Writing Practice

What is stopping you from being a better receiver? Please underline anything pertinent from the list above, and then write your personal a-ha's below:

Notes

3 Aspects of Receiving

The art of receiving and responding has three primary aspects. These are not always sequential, and we may jump from one to the other depending on the circumstance. Each phase has its place, and one is not better than another. These three aspects are: 1) safety, 2) learning, and 3) teaching.

First things first: Avoid harm. If I'm walking through a rough part of town or if someone close to me is angry and yelling, I won't be as open. I'll do what I've learned to do to defend myself. I don't want to live that way all the time. But when life requires me to, I'm glad I know how. Doing this temporarily preserves my energy, so that I can be effective and enjoy life more, once conditions are better.

To steer clear of injury on the Aikido mat, we learn how to fall and roll safely, we get good at blending and being flexible, and we develop skills and resilience to navigate more intense training. This phase is more ego-based, in that it's all about the body and material reality. I need my body to get me around and so I must protect it. Fair enough.

When we feel secure, the second stage moves beyond the ego to make room for something greater. This looks like getting curious. Rather than going through the motions, relating with a family member in habitual ways, I can wonder who this person is today. I can open to learn something new, whether that's about them or me or the world we live in. Being inquisitive requires that we first have our safety needs met. Once safety is a given, a much greater world opens up, and deeper love is possible.

In Aikido training, this stage is the learning stage. As I flow with a more experienced practitioner as she applies a technique to me, I feel how to do it. I let go of my ideas and

I relax my body. I am not in survival, and so I can see more of what's happening in the moment. Neither my fears nor my assumptions run the show.

In the third stage of receiving, we become teachers. In the above example, my senpai (the more experienced student) could teach me by moving her body into the correct position, even a split second before I take her there. In this way, her ukemi draws me to do the technique correctly. If she does her part well, I'll feel like, "Wow, I'm good at Aikido!" It will seem like I threw her, even though she helped me do it.

You know how some people are stubborn, and they have to think something is their idea before they do it? This is where you can "teach" them, perhaps by asking questions that help them find their answer. You're receiving, but at the same time, you are subtly leading them.

Have you ever been oblivious to social cues, and unknowingly acted in a way that offended someone? In this case, if just one person around you models a better way, it helps you adjust yourself without confrontation.

Showing up as a "teacher" all the time is not the goal. The third stage of receiving is not *better* than the first or second. At any given moment, mastery means doing what's needed.

For those who live with constant safety concerns, these must be handled first, and self-preservation should absolutely supersede learning. That said, many people are still protecting themselves from things that happened years ago, which are not happening anymore. We must discern the difference, if we wish to play in the art of love.

Some folks are thirsty for knowledge, and live 24/7 in learning mode even though they are ready to teach. And perpetual teachers may be just as self-centered as those in the first stage. Dropping out of our heads and into our bodies, along with dedicated practice over time, should foster a more instinctive and honest way of being.

When someone has a high level of self-mastery, they exude clarity, and yet their personality is very much intact. When our responses are relevant to the moment, a similar thing happens. Strong energies feel "clean" and are less likely to offend or leave residue. Good Aikido is like this.

Receiving is so much more than either getting what you want or getting invaded. It is a commitment to staying connected, flowing with the dictates of the moment. Truly, it is half of what it means to be alive.

Responding Accurately

Responding accurately is one gift of the healthy feminine. It solves the problems of either being *too nice* or being *too much*. When you respond accurately, there are occasions where softness is needed, other times to be strongly assertive, and moments which require playfulness, disengagement, or something else.

What is accuracy? Accuracy according to what? From the Aikido spirit, the goal is to foster love and life. So, if you're hurting me, love must say "Stop." If your offer feels good to me, love says "Yes, please." If you're clueless with regards to my needs, love gets frustrated. Because love includes no, yes, and everything in between. None of these responses are *wrong* if they're what the moment calls for. And even a "negative" response can increase energy flow if the flow was off prior to that response. Righteous anger or the release of pent-up tears can give us a feeling of "Finally ... freedom!" Freedom is what the masculine ultimately craves, and yet the big love of the Divine feminine may be the gateway.

Keeping in mind the capacity of your partner, your accurate response may be more or less *nice*. Choosing to follow and fall—even when a novice student doesn't have your balance—is an act of grace that aligns with the goal of fostering life force. Slowing down enough for him to figure things out would increase the energy flow between you, and therefore would be an appropriate choice in that moment. Any faster, and he might shut down, causing practice to stop entirely. The same slow pace would rarely be "accurate" for a black belt in good health. Unless she was purposely going in low gear to feel the subtle energy dynamics, her natural flow could feel stifled or dishonored by your snail's pace. Experienced partners tend to enjoy training faster and harder, challenging each other and themselves in appropriate measure.

With both my clients and people I know, I've seen a lot of breakups lately with a common theme. The person leaving the partnership wants to relate at a level they feel the other cannot meet. Often, they complain about the other's lack of emotional capacity and presence. Whether it's Aikido skill or off-mat relational skill, it's normal to yearn to be met at our level. To not be able to do so feels like shutting down a part of ourselves.

On the mat, we not only respond by falling down or flowing with our partner. In the responsive role, we also must attack when given the opportunity. From entering with a strike as partner steps back and drops his sword, to turning back towards the person who just threw you and attacking again, uke has a duty to keep trying.

Remember that in life, the "attack" is not necessarily physical or aggressive. Being responsive in life means we stay awake, and proactively participate when we are called to engage. Just as playing uke on the mat means you both attack and fall down, receptivity off the mat could look like approaching someone if their smile and body language draws you in. It could mean channeling your inspiration into art of some sort. These dynamic actions come through us, as if the wind is at our sails. Even though we initiate, we do so as an answer to life's call.

In this way, Aikido is continuous. It's not so simple to think, "I did my part and now I'm done." Whether your part is the throw or the flow and fall, the goal is to stay connected and martially aware, willingly participating in what's next.

Sometimes you stay upright, continuing to attack where you can. When required, you defer to your partner's movement in a way that not only protects you; it also bolsters him. It is an "I'll do what increases energy for *us*" focus. It's not, "Ok … I'll let you win." While those two may look the same on quick glance, they are and feel very different. One expands life force and the other shuts it down.

What Makes Us Feel Attacked in Life?

While in Aikido practice, *receiving* often means following fairly prescribed movements, such as taking a roll or lowering onto your belly, it gets more confusing off the mat. There are not such clear rules as to what to do in response to a real-life invitation or verbal assault, for instance.

Like our responses in Aikido, our martial attacks are pretty straightforward: punches, grabs, and specific strikes. Off the mat, an attack might translate to any strong energy coming our way. On the part of the attacker, it's an assertive and committed act.

In life, we can feel attacked by intimacy or surprise as much as by anger. And so, partner's punch might represent:

- That school bully or family member calling you names
- A love interest asking you out
- Your significant other pushing for closeness
- Your child crying, grabbing your legs
- A challenging client, co-worker, or community member
- A driver honking and tailgating
- For a surfer, a big wave (or translate to your favorite hobby)
- Someone throwing you a surprise party

With each of the above, the same knee-jerk reactions tend to come forth: we fight, flee, or freeze. To do Aikido off the mat, we must change these tendencies and instead align, protect ourselves as needed, and redirect the energy in a life-giving way.

How to do this gets quite interesting! Aikido teaches us alternative ways to handle attacks, and I'll share what they are in the coming chapters.

Finding Connection

How often do we choose to connect when hit with conflict in life? Most of us instead avoid, attack back, or defend or push to get our point across. We commonly misjudge connection as agreement or even defeat. Quite the contrary, victory is more likely once we see what the other person is seeing.

I filed an insurance claim recently, and after receiving a payout, I believed the company owed me more money. After going back and forth with them about it, I asked to speak with the manager. When we spoke on the phone, she empathized with my position. She told me she'd do the same as me, if she were in my shoes. And by the time she explained why the company's policies did not allow them to pay more, I was seeing her as an ally and not as an enemy. While I wish I got more insurance money, I applaud her skill in standing her ground without alienating a customer.

I remember Ikeda Sensei repeating these two words with his Japanese accent: "Catch it." As he called various people up to strike, he insisted you must first join with your attacker's energy before successfully applying technique. The Japanese have a word for this connection: *musubi*.

What if we could hear and relate with the other person before sharing our perspective? What would it cost us? Usually, nothing, with much to be gained.

In my life and that of my clients, this is nearly essential if we wish to sway someone. The more stubborn they are, the more delicate this art. Have you ever met that person whose rigidity melted as soon as you didn't fight back? Do not underestimate the power of your calm center to transform others, simply by providing a reflection.

If they're dangerous or if you must respond quickly, then perhaps stopping to listen is inappropriate. In this case, is there still an opportunity to connect? Aikido offers a range of ways, and each of them starts with what I'm about to cover.

Redirecting Tension

First things first: Keep yourself safe. You can't receive if you're not safe, and you must be able to receive in order to redirect. And therefore, this first principle of receiving (safety) is a must if you wish for higher love. Meeting other people wearing rose-colored glasses, with your feet off the ground, is not lasting or effective.

For example, what would knock you down on a bad day will barely touch you when you're anchored. In the face of unwarranted attacks on your character, not responding lets the truth speak for itself. Maintaining your strong position is not unkind. It is what frees you to share your energy for mutual benefit.

In learning new Aikido moves, frequently beginners will second-guess each step. "Just move your body," I remind them. Starting simply with repositioning ensures that you won't be hit. This alone can throw the other person off guard, and it may require only a small movement. A strike quickly loses meaning once the target isn't where the attacker expected!

In daily life, this is such an easy thing, but most of us forget. We get so wrapped up in the attack that we forget the big picture and our power in responding. Whether receiving an invitation or an insult, we limit the flow of love when we become a deer in the headlights, staring down that thing coming our way. *That* thing is only one thing happening in any given moment! Your whole being is much bigger than the person you think you are when you're triggered.

That said, we may react from our wounding without thinking, in moments of stress. Or we get tripped up with thoughts like:

"Oh my gosh, what am I going to say?"

"I don't want to hurt her feelings."

"He said ____ about me, but really he is a ____ himself!"

"I'm not ____; I'm actually _____."

"What if I do ____ and ____ happens? Yikes!!!"

In Aikido class, I'll often illustrate this by having one person grab another's wrist. If the person being grabbed focuses on the tension, and starts fighting to get her wrist loose, she misses the opportunity to do so many other things. The truth is, only her wrist is occupied. The rest of her body is free to move. Her eyes and mind are able to perceive the entire situation. All she has to do is slide into a new spot, letting her partner have that wrist. Assuming his grip is secure, he will follow her movement. In this way, she can position herself to take his balance and throw him down, at which time he'll have to let go of her wrist anyway. It will become completely incidental.

This strategy, which we call *getting off the line*, works wonders off the mat with certain personality types who thrive on your attention and will do most anything to get it. Just letting them do what they do without giving it any energy will set you up better, even if it's challenging in the moment. Not only does moving out of the way protect you, but you may also see a different vantage point from your new position. And staying out of the drama offers you more choices.

One of my clients faced regular verbal assaults from her partner. She found herself constantly anxious, wrapped up in arguments that stole both her confidence and focus. I was disheartened to see how this drained her energy.

"Don't play ball on his court," I told her. "No one is winning this game. If he makes an accusation that isn't true, don't defend yourself or blame him. Come back to the facts, or perhaps listen and ask him what *he* needs." This is one way we can join with the energy behind someone's attack.

If someone in your life acts in a hurtful way, you can argue or comply, but there are other options. In extreme cases, you may need to remove yourself—temporarily or permanently. Most of the time, you can use humor, ask a question, or find another artful means of shifting the dynamic.

3 Ways to Handle Conflict

Aikido offers us three primary ways to handle conflict. On or off the mat, when something comes at you that seems intimidating, you can do any of these things to diffuse the situation. They are:

1. *Irimi*—entering. Dive right into it, face it, and handle it directly.
2. *Tenkan*—turning. Get out of the way and let the momentum pass before you handle the situation.
3. *Tenshin*—drawing. Reposition yourself so you can safely bring your partner to your own center, disrupting his balance as you do.

Let's discuss how we might apply these in everyday life. I'll start with irimi.

Irimi—Entering in Directly

Let's say you have someone new at your workplace. Not realizing, they do something that negatively affects you or the business. An irimi approach would be to speak up right away—before they have developed a habit and before you have any pent-up tension around the situation. It just happened! The situation is fresh, and it's easy to correct. Assert yourself, enter in, and face it directly.

Imagine you are dating someone new or beginning a friendship. The other person regularly expects you to be available at a moment's notice. Irimi-style, you could say something like, "Hey, I'd love to see you soon. How does next week look?" In this early stage of acquaintance, you are teaching the other person how to treat you. While making yourself available 24/7 may be tempting when you're first getting to know them, how are you going to feel about doing so in six months or a year? Irimi it now and set yourself up for success.

If you've spent time around children, you have likely seen the benefits of irimi. For instance, there's no reason to let your son hit his brother several times before you say anything. This is a time to assert yourself, not to assume the kids will figure it out. Before someone gets too hurt, before you lose your patience, and prior to your son deciding you're ok with this—step in and speak up. Children respond very well to calm, clear direction. They have so much life force and are new to their bodies. Therefore, healthy boundaries give them a sense of safety that boosts confidence and positive self-expression.

During the writing of this book, my daughter and I went to a national park over a holiday weekend. The hiking trails were quite crowded, to the point where we both had to pass slower hikers and also allow the faster folks to pass us. I didn't mind stopping to let someone go ahead, but what irked me were the "tailgaters." They'd walk inches behind us without asking to pass. Did they think this was more polite? Were they deliberately trying to annoy us? Did they even realize what they were doing? In any case, I would have preferred they had the foresight to assess their speed compared to ours, and shouted out, "Excuse me," irimi-fashion. This direct, thoughtful assertion would have given us plenty of time to graciously move aside.

Experiencing what I did validated my sense that most people are quite uncomfortable with conflict, even where avoiding it feels worse and causes more problems. If this is how so many folks approach hiking among strangers, I wonder how many family matters could be solved if people spoke early and directly? How refreshing it would be if more unconscious, avoidant, passive-aggressive behaviors could be replaced with the respect that irimi offers! I believe, with this shift, people could also get what they want more easily.

On the Aikido mat, an irimi step is a purposeful move forward, without hesitation. You have to be very aware to do this. The more you master it, the more you avoid situations that would have become worse if you were more tentative.

Tenkan—Letting the Intensity Pass before Handling a Situation

My daughter and I were on the way to meet her dad, and she was nervous. "Mama, what are we going to do about that thing he said?" (He had taken a stance on something that affected her, and neither she nor I agreed with him.)

"Don't worry about it. I'm gonna tenkan it," I said. My daughter does Aikido, so she understood. "We're just not going to bring it up. We'll talk about other things."

He and I were supposed to have a meeting about that subject a week or two later, and he cancelled. Just as I thought, by the time he brought it up a few weeks after that, he had already dropped his agenda and decided to go along with what my daughter and I wanted.

This worked because I know his personality. Not everything he talks about pans out, so I've learned to "wait and see."

Ever met the "bark is worse than his bite" type? If you engage with the bark, you waste a lot of energy, because it inevitably changes.

With any personality, you could wait out the tension if you know they're in a bad mood, haven't had enough sleep, or aren't yet seeing the situation accurately. I also suggest tenkan when someone is aggressive, if you don't feel you can safely protect yourself.

In our Aikido black belt tests, we must defend against multiple challengers. And in this *randori* practice, it's completely acceptable to just move your body sometimes. You don't have to take every adversary to the ground every time; sometimes you can just push them off and slide out of the way.

Faced with strong energy in daily life, the safety you need may be emotional, physical, or energetic. Rather than setting yourself up to be hurt or overwhelmed, find some space so you can give yourself what you need.

Keeping the idea that intimacy may be as scary as a physical attack, you could tenkan when someone is coming on strong—even just to buy yourself some time to see how you feel. Use tenkan with a salesman, with your pushy mother-in-law, or with your boisterous child.

This type of self-care can be surprisingly powerful, as compared to using physical strength. As you stay light and relaxed when someone is fired up, your feminine energy magnetizes their masculine into your sphere of softness. The more they focus on you, the more they feel what you feel and will go where you are. However, your priority is yourself; it's not about changing them. This can really puzzle someone who's used to willing their way at any cost. It's not what they expect, and yet it feels surprisingly good.

I shared the example earlier of letting your partner have your wrist, turning, and then using your whole body to throw him. In in-class demonstrations, I'll point at his grab and say, "This is not dangerous. *He* is what's dangerous." As I gesture towards his face and whole body, students frequently laugh in recognition. He might threaten a punch or kick just to illustrate the point. Tenkan, turning away from the line of danger, is a highly effective strategy that reframes and dissolves conflict.

Tenshin—Drawing Your Partner
to Your Place of Strength

Tenshin neither enters in nor turns and lets things be. Tenshin says, "You want me? You can have me, but I get a say in how this goes." Tenshin says, "Let's do this together."

On the Aikido mat, a tenshin movement is a diagonal step back that requires your partner to come a little further in to "get you." It works because they are already heading your way. By the time they find you, you've brought them to your own center, and their momentum has dissipated.

My client was frustrated when her boyfriend didn't express daily affection the way she wanted. Realizing that her neediness wasn't helping matters, she said, "I think I need to be more bitchy." While I thought she was on the right track, I expressed caution.

"Remember when you just focused on you and your happiness, and he came towards you?" I asked. "Remember how you responded nonchalantly because you were already happy and secure, and he was a bonus? That's what works for you, not bitchiness. I don't think that he'd respond well to that."

"No, he doesn't," she admitted.

The difference between tenshin and manipulation is this. You focus on being where *you* feel good. It's more about you than it is about controlling the other person. If you're primarily moving as a power play, they'll feel it and will either retreat or fight. Whereas, if you're having fun, they're eager to dive in deeper and have fun with you.

In Aikido we have a saying, "Push, don't pull." There's a fine line between "drawing" and "pulling." With any good Aikido, we are inviting and collaborating from a place of conviction that we've already won. On the mat, by the time you try to pull someone into place, you've already lost. When you're desperate to regain control, your efforts are futile. You've lost the impact you might have had on your partner, and you've lost the Aikido.

In everyday life, people manipulate because they feel weak and don't believe they can win any other way. But acting from a shaky foundation doesn't pay off. If you find yourself maneuvering while grasping to save face, I suggest pausing and finding your own center. At times, that may mean disengaging from an interaction or slowing things way down until you regain balance. This takes patience, but in the long run, it both saves time and improves your relationships exponentially. It rarely works to act from a place of panic or brute force.

Tenshin is highly dynamic and comes with a feeling of, "Surprise, I'm not where you thought I was!" To the uke, who attacks and then finds her target has moved, it feels like a fun ride. When this is done well, the attacker tends to wonder, "How did I end up here?" even when she knows the moves.

Optimizing Your Timing

Timing is critical if you are to optimize your opportunities. In life, there are windows where certain actions are favored. At less advantageous times, it's best to lay low and wait until conditions are better. Paying attention, we can move with more grace and fulfillment. When we overly attempt to control the timing of things, we generally find more conflict, stagnation, and/or regrets due to missed potentials.

I am often told I call people at the perfect time. Listening inward for *right timing*, we can live more in flow, with a greater sense of aliveness. Everyone involved tends to feel better, and more can be accomplished. Life feels both expansive and peaceful here. When we're living in Divine time, we don't feel the constriction of time.

When I have some unscheduled hours, I follow my instincts and do the activities that feel right when I imagine doing them. It's a great way to conserve energy! On occasion when I override these instincts, people are busy, businesses are closed, calls go unanswered, or other obstacles present.

Have you ever brought up a sensitive topic when the other person just didn't have space, or wasn't in the mood? Or have you reacted to a message before you thought it through, and wished too late that you could unsend? There's no win-win here! It's more of a lose-lose—as the other person feels overwhelmed or annoyed, and your desire to connect gets thwarted.

This is not to say we should walk on eggshells and always accommodate other people's moods. This can perpetuate toxic dynamics. Yet even the most enlightened humans are more or less available at various times, and we serve everyone involved when we roll with that.

Just as you can conduct yourself on the mat to either speed up the interaction or buy yourself time, you can do the same in personal relationships. For one thing, you can respectfully request to schedule time to talk, if you have a burning need but know it's not time to speak in the moment. Conversely, if you are feeling pushed and need more space, you can ask for time and/or plan to meet later when you feel more ready.

In Aikido training, we learn to join with and redirect the momentum of whatever comes our way. If we're too late in responding, we either end up fighting or find there's nothing to work with anymore. If we jump the gun, our reactions don't make sense because the attack's energy hasn't built up enough yet. Anytime our timing is off, our choices can feel out of context or jarring to the other party.

We should not beat ourselves up, though, if we fail to act or act at the wrong time. On the mat, we can sometimes turn a situation around if we keep moving. Perhaps just a few seconds later, or maybe by adjusting our body position, an opening presents itself that wasn't there before.

Similarly, keeping our chin up in life means we'll see the opportunity just past the one we missed. Shrinking in defeat is a guaranteed-lose situation. Remaining resilient and staying present, we continue to honor the life force within and around ourselves. Maybe right after what you just lost, there is someone or something even better. Your wakeful confidence will help you see this when it appears.

Slow Down, Find the Pause

Whether we're beginning Aikido or stepping into any new venture, anxiety can make us jumpy. Talking a mile a minute, over-functioning, or not stopping to rest does not hasten the achievement of a goal. Grabbing hands and frantically moving feet any which way, attempting to perfect a movement, we only exacerbate confusion. Besides the obvious physical errors, if you're not giving yourself enough space, how do you imagine the other person will feel? Of course, it's completely understandable to be nervous with a new relationship, job, or situation. So how do we slow down and breathe here?

Facing physical attack, in a safe context like Aikido class, is a quick study in relaxing under pressure. As we meet the strike while simultaneously moving our body out of reach, we can redirect the attack's direction.

For example, if my partner faces me head-on and grabs my wrist, I can affect her center by turning my hips and center 90 degrees, keeping my hands in front of my waist. Since she's attached to me, she moves too. Now, she may still have my wrist, but she's stretched out and easy to throw. In this moment, time apparently stops. I've got her, so there's no rush to the finish line. I can patiently execute the technique. I have learned to locate, and then move from this sweet spot.

In any endeavor, impatience rarely wins. Especially in heated situations, a well-timed pause can actually speed things up. So, if you're unsure how to handle an argument or opportunity, meet it graciously, and then shift a bit to buy yourself time. The moment to move is the moment you feel you don't have to, and yet still have the option.

Wait too long and it will change, as things always do. Yet there is value in pausing long enough to feel the potency of these moments. To do so means you will connect from a sense of fullness, from the love that you are. It feels like catching a wave. It feels like dancing in perfect flow.

Aikido is based on generosity of spirit, and so any kind of *grasping* is incongruent. If I am united with the life force, where is there to go? If I am one with the Universe, how can anything oppose me? While this sounds lofty, it is worth meditating on.

In both relationships and practical matters, you can fake it until you make it and see what happens. Slow down— and see if you end up speeding up. It's ok if you mostly fail. As soon as this clicks once, you won't be able to convince yourself it's not possible. Your felt experience will deepen your faith.

While those who lean towards laziness must learn to act, most of us need to de-stress and trust more. There's rarely a need to force things. Practice staying relaxed. As long as you're on the right track, know that there will be a moment where success comes easily. When you can, wait to act until victory is assured. If you were planning a wedding or large event, would you want it now or would you want it right? If your child is screaming and hungry, would you talk him out of his mood or would you feed him?

When any of us are fed, our capacity to relate expands greatly. Beyond receiving well and making sure we're nurtured—both physically and otherwise—it's also about re-membering our inherent fullness.

Though many people have low self-worth or even con-fuse self-effacement with humility, Aikido reminds us of our Divine nature. To move from the lie of weakness is a disservice to all life. Instead, we should live from dignity and share from overflow. Finding even a spark of this within you will spiral out and spiral back.

Proper Distance

Years ago, my boyfriend of one month called me to ask how I felt about him moving to my area. We'd met when he was traveling in Colorado and had, so far, spent two weekends together. "If you want to do that for you, that's great. But please don't do it just for me," I replied.

He said he wouldn't. And because his target town was over an hour from me, he suggested, "I could stay with you on the weeks you don't have your daughter."

Yikes! I instantly felt claustrophobic. My non-parenting weeks were like gold to me, where I caught up on work and all things personal. Wasn't it a little early to move in together half the time? I expressed uncertainty on that idea, but said we could keep seeing each other.

We agreed I would fly to his city a month later to help him pack up, and then drive to Colorado together. While he did a number of kind things, such as pay for my plane ticket and fix up a bike so we could ride together during my visit (he knew I loved to bike), I suddenly felt like I'd become his wife. Helping to pick up the U-Haul, packing his house of 12 years in less than a week's time, and cleaning and organizing (let's just say those were not his strong suits) suddenly killed the courtship. He was a nice enough guy, and perhaps it was good that I learned so much about him early on. That said, this felt way too soon to tackle something big like an interstate move together. Live and learn.

In Aikido we have the concept of *maai*, or "proper distance." Though it applies to all aspects of our practice, it's quite notable in sword work. There, improper spacing can result in poking someone in the eye, missing your mark entirely, or overshooting and rendering your cut useless while putting yourself in danger.

Beginner Aikidoka (Aikido practitioners) are often surprised by the closeness required to fall safely. Moving right with him and tucking your head into your partner's shoulder, for example, will keep you from getting smacked in the nose during certain throws. And some techniques can only be executed if you slide in against your partner's body, which takes some getting used to! In other cases, we can only take someone's balance if we step away and get leverage.

My ex-boyfriend and I saw each other for a few months after he moved to Colorado, and then parted after acknowledging we were looking for different things. I appreciated his desire for partnership, but I didn't want to be put in the box of his vision, especially before really getting to know one another. Given where we were at in that process, our distance was too close to support a union based in free-flowing life force.

In anything from early acquaintance to long-term partnership, we are constantly negotiating our distance. Too close and the fire goes out. Too far and we lose sight of each other. This varies from day to day, year to year, and what is needed continually changes. We must stay attuned and flexible and honest.

For a first date, driving separately to a neutral public place might feel best. Diving in deeper, inviting them to your home could be a beautiful gesture of growing closeness. After a romantic weekend, time apart for each person to re-ground and integrate may be in order.

Some couples prefer to sleep in separate beds, even when the passion between them is strong. They may just rest better having their own spaces. Others enjoy different hobbies and interests, especially after years or decades of doing things as a unit. Done well, this can fan the flames of romance, as each individual brings their happy and full self to the partnership. We each deserve to keep our own inner spark alive. And in doing so, we inspire and magnetize our loved ones.

Relationships have their cycles, and a temporary out breath will not extinguish a solid connection. Many things such as illness, the death of a family member, a work project, or a period of inner growth can increase the distance between two people. It happens with friends, family—all types of relationships, really—as much as between life partners. It is not to be feared; in fact, allowing these cycles is one key to a truly vital, long-term relationship.

Maybe a certain family member, client, or friend is difficult. Perhaps they trigger you. You can find an appropriate distance so that the dynamic works for you. For example, stay at a hotel instead of at your brother's house. Let the client know which days and times you're available, and your terms of engagement. Pick an end time and let your friend know it's been nice chatting after the hour is up.

For some relationships, or during certain phases, distance can also grow too vast. A common example are couples that become roommates after having kids. They blink and another year of diapers, soccer games, and birthday parties has gone by. Unless they see what's happening and close the distance early on—for instance, by scheduling dates or by hiring help they need to avoid exhaustion—many of these folks find their marriage hard to save.

If you're anxious about what's happening at work or with a family member, ask. Talk to your kids, if you have them, so they feel safe talking to you. And if you're on a date and you're hoping your love interest will make a move, lean in.

You'll rarely have to cut people out of your life when you master maai. Nor will you lose sight of those you love. Keeping appropriate distance helps you make the most of each interaction, every time.

Setting Yourself Up for Success

First impressions impact whatever comes next. In Aikido practice, it is no different. How you begin determines how you finish.

For instance, the one being attacked learns not to be passive. I teach my students to have an "in charge" attitude before the other person begins to strike. This is a prerequisite if you wish to effectively handle the attack. Like a seed sprouting beneath the earth, winning or losing is determined before the technique is even perceptible to the physical eye.

Imagine being able to secure your success prior to whatever would otherwise intimidate you. In your daily life, what would it be like to be habitually ready, instead of getting blindsided by whatever comes your way?

I am asked sometimes if I've ever used Aikido in a real-life, physical conflict. Well, I have not been in a street fight, thank goodness. But in addition to avoiding injury when I slipped on ice or on a moving bus (I instinctively knew how to fall safely), I believe Aikido protects me simply because I walk with greater confidence and presence. Perpetrators have been shown to seek apparently weak victims, and they will not approach where they think they will lose or get caught.

When we want to, we can both invite someone to approach us *and* set ourselves up to handle it with confidence. For example, as you extend an arm, you could imagine it's full of breath. When your partner grabs that arm, he can feel you, and your energetic presence makes you less likely to collapse under his force.

There is an artful way to offer energy without being the aggressor in life. You can flirt, inquire, or show up with warmth. This signals those around that you're open to conversation and to their invitations, aka attacks.

By contrast, let's say you're at an event, shrinking against the wall. Probably, fewer people will talk with you, and those who do may come across in a dominant way. Your conversations may not lead you anywhere you want to go. Alternately, if you show up talking loudly about yourself and stepping on toes, you may push people away.

Do you initially meet people with appreciation, antagonism, or curiosity? Notice how relationships pan out depending on their beginnings.

In Aikido, being centered and ready makes it exponentially more likely that you'll react to a strike with similar openness. Beginners are often surprised by how lightly and fluidly an experienced student meets their attack. You don't need force when you feel competent and have solid technique. All this sets the stage for whether you'll emerge victorious. And once you get the opening right, you have already won and have many choices of what to do next. Learning to do this significantly reduces stress, as it allows you to slow down. It gives the overwhelmed mind a place to focus.

Many of us feel we have to manage everything 24/7. From here, we become frazzled and feel helpless to get anything right. If we can just keep attending to one step at a time as it presents itself, the rest will fall into place. Particularly, starting each thing well will expand our experience of time.

Don't Keep Stopping to Analyze or Make It Perfect

Driving a car or riding a bike, have you ever started to turn right, then realized you meant to go left instead? When this happens, it's safer to turn right and go around the block than it is to veer left into traffic. However frustrating, turning right may be the only possibility, if roads are busy.

In Aikido training, we sometimes find ourselves doing things we didn't mean to do. If I intend to step behind my partner for a technique, and instead start moving in front, it's better to keep going to the front rather than to confuse him, muddy things up, and risk injuries.

A good performing artist will masterfully make a mistake look like he meant to do it. He doesn't stop and tell the band to rewind and start again two measures back. He'll cue them with body language and make up new lyrics if he has to. Most listeners will have no idea anything went wrong! I tell my Aikido students sometimes to pretend they're part of a band playing to an audience, for this reason.

In relationships of all types, the energetic dance with your partner doesn't naturally stop. However, it will short circuit when you constantly pull out the microscope. Of course, do your best to understand and remedy mistakes, and keep responding and directing energy in a life-affirming way. That may or may not look like what you *meant* to do, or what you *should* do in any given moment. And that's ok. Just don't stop and hide until you think you can make it all perfect.

One of my spiritual teachers used to joke with his students about how "green" they were. Green was symbolic of growth. His comments were a nice way of pointing out that the person was going through a lot of change. As long as we were working through our stuff, though, he didn't worry about us. He said he only got concerned when we got stuck.

Continuous movement is not about speeding up. In fact, if you need to slow down so you feel comfortable to keep moving, do that. If you're enjoying getting to know someone but are uncertain how far you want to take it, then pace yourself. This goes not only for romance, but also for friendships or work relationships. You don't have to attend to everyone's demands right this second, nor do you need to indulge all your own impulses. If you feel overwhelmed, you also don't have to freeze.

Most of us are either too frenetic or too stagnant. The antidote is to notice one bite-sized action you can take right now. One by one, these simple choices add up to a masterful life. These make sense and feel easy, and they keep both your energy and your relationships healthy and flowing.

Embodied Relating, from the Ground Up

Most of us live life from the head and upper body, and we try to understand something new mentally first, before doing it. We focus on what's flashy and fancy and we miss the foundation, which often seems mundane and less important. It's not.

Becoming an Aikido teacher required me to really get clear on the movements, so I can break them down for students. The more we practice *kihon waza* (basic technique), including footwork drills, the more we see recognizable themes in even the most dynamic Aikido. Inevitably, most of us first waste a lot of time getting things wrong and making things harder than they are, because we're dazzled by complexity over roots. The deeper I get into my Aikido, the simpler it seems.

While at higher levels there is much nuance in our practice, it's important to know the basics first, before you can easily expand into more advanced training. There is that saying, *you have to know the rules before you can break the rules.*

Our culture wants everything fast and now, and while technology enables this to a degree, much depth is lost. We live in a world where live contact is increasingly replaced with texting, automated systems, and robots. It's a costly delusion to think this can replace human interaction. We can swipe right and left all day long, and still go to sleep lonely.

Beginning a romantic relationship slowly lays the groundwork for success by making sure you know one another well before getting more involved. Many experts advise dating—even starting as friends—for a period of time before becoming intimate. A year or more is often recommended before moving in, getting married, or making any long-term commitments.

I have also heard the advice to hire slowly in business. And nurturing our children when they're young sets the stage for them to grow into well-adjusted adults.

When you prepare for anything important, you show up grounded and it goes better. This can be as simple as getting a good night's sleep, eating well, or organizing your packing list for a trip.

When I returned to Aikido after a long break, I saw it from mid-life eyes versus the eyes of youth. I saw it at a time when social media had become mainstream, and people were stepping up as "gurus" just because they had a few good soundbites or had taken a 90-day class. It turned me off. And then looking at my former training partners who'd achieved multiple black belt ranks, I regretted dropping the practice. No amount of shine and sparkle could replace decades of lived experience, having shown up on both your best and worst days. I got it. I started again and vowed to hold steady.

Aikido teaches us to drop what we think we know, to surrender our expectations, and to reel our minds in from trying to race ahead and protect us. None of this works in physical practice. It just gets in the way of actual connection with a real-life human who does not share your head space.

What we share on the mat may appear otherworldly, and we are in fact going for that mystical sense of oneness. Yet, it happens because of a real-time, embodied energy exchange. When we start with a solid foundation, we can relax our thinking and meet one another from our being-selves. This makes way for Divine union to occur.

Put Your Hips Down Last

In getting to know someone new, we chance disappointment when we commit fully before we know what we're diving into. Whether it's a friendship, romance, business contact—or anything you might commit to—it's healthy to take things step by step. Caution with new people or endeavors does not indicate fear or over-rigidity; in fact, these emotions more likely go along with rushing.

Secure people innately know this. Their self-worth would settle for nothing less. They suss things out before they give themselves fully, because they believe their energy is valuable.

Certain Aikido techniques end with uke lowering down onto his belly. As these techniques are applied to him, he must stay nimble. He progressively lowers his knees and shoulders, and *only* when it's clear that he can't get back up shall he put his hips down. At any moment until that point, he could pop back up if nage lets up on the pressure.

Our hips are what allow us to move or not move. As soon as we put them down, we've surrendered. Beginner Aikidoka will often either resist or just flop on the ground. There is a happy medium. We learn to move towards the floor, all the while keeping our options open as long as possible. If nage lets up on the pressure, we can pop back up and attack again—*as long as our hips aren't down.*

Of course, some folks keep their options open too much in life, and in doing so, they may use others. Self-worth is different from selfishness. If you never commit or give in, your personal evolution may come from consciously doing so where appropriate. If you're prone to giving 100% before discerning whether you should, perhaps practice taking more time.

On and off the mat, we must recognize where the moment dictates that we concede, and then do so willingly. This is an act of strength, and an affirmation of both ourselves and our relationships.

The more we go at a methodical pace, the more we create long-term wins. Slowing down helps us to be appropriately open and comfortable. With this approach, we sense what we're entering into more clearly. And just like lowering your body on the mat, you'll have a few *outs* before you take that big step *all in*.

Moving from Integrity

Alignment in our bodies and lives gives us more power. In Aikido, as we throw with our left arm, we step with our left leg. Whole body and whole being move together in a fully committed act. This force is felt by anyone near, and it's one reason little people can throw big people effectively. This is integrity, not dividing ourselves. It also makes us trustable. It inspires partners to follow cooperatively.

How can we expect to feel aligned with other people, or with a job or place—anything really—if we aren't aligned within ourselves? If you find yourself saying, "Part of me feels X, and part of me feels Y," that's a good indicator to ask yourself, "What do I really feel?" and to let the answer be ok.

Finding integrity may seem to require sacrifice, for we live in a world of having your cake and eating it too. Making simple, aligned choices is underrated. Yet, I see people becoming happier when they do. Paradoxically, this can give us more time and energy and abundance on all levels. Most people, though, are dizzy trying to divide themselves in a million pieces all the time in fleeting hopes of "living the dream."

When we say one thing and do another, or when our actions are inconsistent and confusing, we are not just pissing people off. We are leaking power. We are disturbing love and denying life. In a similar way, our Aikido techniques don't work when our energy and actions aren't integrated. We can blame the other person, or we can look honestly and adjust our side of things.

If we attract those who aren't consistent, they may simply not have learned how to be. Someone who grew up with indirect, unreliable caregivers has no reference point for communicating from inner clarity. A beginner in Aikido whose technique is clumsy is not a bad person. In dealing with people like this, your best bet is to keep your own integrity. Don't overly explain or make them wrong. State your needs or requests as is appropriate. Otherwise, simply offer your grounded, clear, and accurate actions. This will give them the opportunity to match you. Inspire their transformation, rather than forcing them into it.

If you know how to show up as your best and don't do it, you cannot blame the other person when you fall down on top of each other, or when your relationship blows up. Your lack of alignment will be reflected back eventually!

One sneaky way we compromise our alignment is through overextending. It can be hard to spot, in that we may tell ourselves we are helping the other person, even rescuing them. We may develop a victim story that says, "I did so much for you; how dare you betray me." In many cases, we have betrayed ourselves and they're just reflecting it back. On the mat, this could look like bending over instead of maintaining proper posture. Don't get mad if you compromise your stance, and then the other person throws you!

At times, your integrity might look like *not* accommodating someone (or not falling down for them), when you feel that doing so would be a disservice to you or them. In other cases, your generosity and grace in the face of their ignorance is what allows them to learn. Knowing when to do what can take years or decades, and this is why we practice. On and off the mat, this reveals mastery far beyond technical knowledge.

Living in integrity all the time is a huge feat, and very few of us have perfected it. To support you in finding this within yourself, I'll offer an exercise in the next section.

Writing Practice:
Finding Your Alignment Within

Write down your answers to the following questions:

1. Where do you feel conflicted in life?

2. Is there anyone else in your past or present environment who has opinions or feelings about what you're conflicted about, or something similar?

3. Do you have any memories, experiences, or beliefs that may be influencing you or fueling this inner conflict?

4. What are your core values and priorities? Can these help you resolve the conflict?

5. Is there something obvious that needs attention today? Even if you don't make any big decisions or final conclusions yet, where can you find peace in this moment?

Notes

Trusting Your Center

The more we master Aikido, the less we worry about the mechanics, and the more we simply move from body-knowing. Knowing that your partner is attached to you and trusting in your own technique, you adopt an attitude of, "I don't care if you're coming with me or not." It sounds flippant and uncaring, but it actually comes across as the opposite.

Being overly focused on the other person makes us jumpy, needy, or pushy. Without faith in ourselves, we tend to use muscle (on the mat), angry words (off the mat), or force. Even the best of us may resort to manipulation—or just run away—when we don't believe we can have something. None of this feels good to those around us.

By contrast, self-confidence and self-worth make us kinder. When we approach Aikido from this space, we initiate movements from our center and whole body. This feels much gentler than slapping someone in the face. It's also way easier, especially when you are smaller than your partner, or appear to have a disadvantage. This is not about controlling things outside of yourself, or things beyond your control. It's just that whoever—or whatever—comes your way has to orchestrate around you. This is how you get what you want without fighting, manipulating, or convincing. You make the rules about what happens in your space. If someone attacks you, bring them into your sphere where you choose the terms of engagement. Your presence is your best protection. Once we realize the power we have spiritually, there is not much to fight about.

This principle works not only physically, but also energetically. Let's say someone is thinking about you a lot and you find them "in your head." Fighting or resisting this does no good! You don't want to keep thinking about them, so how do you handle this type of thing?

When I started meditating as a young adult, I'd find my dad's energy in my head most every time I checked. After attempting many strategies that did not work, I started dressing him up in a pink tutu in my mind's eye, and then he'd bolt! To be clear, he could wear whatever he wanted in real life. But in *my* head, that was what he had to wear. Between focusing on my own sphere of influence and finding amusement instead of resistance, this former "invasion" became a non-issue.

Not only do we typically overstress and miss the mark in defending ourselves, most of us also strive ineffectively to achieve our goals. We worry too much about what to do, wear, or say. We misperceive our worth and do backflips to "get" what is already inside us. Most of us are too hard on ourselves, and so muscle our way through life. Aikido quickly reveals these bad habits.

Because we use our hips and center to overcome an attacker, small people can be very skilled at Aikido. The founder was only 5'2"! I sometimes ask my kids' class if they think he became a master because of his muscles. "No!" they shout. They are likely better than we adults at really feeling where Aikido comes from.

We would all do well to adopt a child-like spirit, and to stop relying on our size, status, or assumptions. What we experience outside ourselves reflects what is inside. It's dumfounding to stop fighting and suddenly realize all we've ever wanted. Yet these miracles happen regularly for those who learn how to harness them.

Trusting Each Other

A secure connection requires that both people participate. You could do your part perfectly, but if your partner disengages, all that's left is your own composure. She might relate with you with amazing attunement. But if you jerk her around, she'll rarely feel secure or good, even if she has the skill to make your relationship look perfect on the surface.

Trust breeds trust, and mistrust brings more mistrust. Aikido is based in mutual trust, which takes getting used to for most of us! Beginners can sometimes be tough with their partners, perhaps because they think martial artists should be. On a deeper level, they're rough because they aren't sure of themselves yet. These same folks tend to turn away as a technique is applied to them, and I get it. How do they know that their training partners will take care of them? Ideally, Aikido class is a safe space to practice trusting.

In daily life, we unfortunately should not trust everyone all the time. However, so much love goes unreceived, and so much love is ungiven when we guard ourselves inappropriately. Creativity and connection vanish in the face of mistrust.

In the workplace, employees who are micromanaged typically express resentment, apathy, and/or a desire to leave their job. Whereas, being trusted tends to inspire loyalty, happiness, and better performance. While some initial screening or ongoing checks may be needed, these should not be the focal point if good relations and creativity are to flourish.

Let's say you hold back from sharing your heart with someone dear to you, for fear of how they'll respond. You likely just shortchanged both yourself and the other person, and you both missed an opportunity to love. Most of us are starving for true intimacy, and I'm talking beyond the bedroom. We crave safe places to be vulnerable, where we can be all that we are with another human.

Clients often come to me complaining about certain people in their lives, not seeing their own potential to affect the situation. We can have our needs met much more often when we simply voice them, respectfully. You doing so helps reveal their character. If they respond in a dismissive or uncaring way, you haven't lost much, and you've gained valuable clarity. Most people, though, are good at heart, and they will respond kindly even if they aren't willing or able to give you what you ask for. So, unless that person has already proven to you that they're abusive or dismissive, you shouldn't have to lock your heart up in steel from the beginning.

I recommend assuming your partner/friend/co-worker/boss/client/family member—whomever you're relating with—would like to support you if they could. I suggest sharing openly what you think and feel, as relates to this person and your dynamic. Of course, discern when and how much to share, but practice *feeling* trust and freedom—versus fear and closure—as your baseline.

The following exercise will support you in developing healthy trust.

Writing Practice:
Developing Trust

Answer the following questions:

1. Where and how am I not trusting in myself, my life, or relationships?

2. Why not?

3. What would it look like if I trusted myself 10% more this week?

4. In what ways (if any) am I inappropriately mistrustful of other people, and in what ways (if any) am I inappropriately trusting?

5. Why?

6. What would it look like if I trusted another person 10% more this week? Or how might I practice more discernment if I am too trusting?

7. What good do I imagine coming from my trusting myself and/or others more appropriately? How might this benefit my life?

Notes

Keep Your Hands—and Awareness—in Front of You

Trusting your partner comes more naturally when you're in a strong position. And when you're weak or uncentered, it makes more sense to—literally and figuratively—watch your back.

On the Aikido mat, keeping your hands in front of you is one indicator of being ready and attentive. You're not leaving an important part of yourself where you can't see it, any more than you'd leave a small child or your valuable things out on the street.

This is most notable when one partner grabs the other from behind. If he gets her wrists and pulls them down and back, it's difficult for her to defend herself. In receiving this type of attack, she should instead move in such a way that her hands stay forward of her center *before and as he grabs*. This way, she dictates how he may and may not connect with her. He has to extend further to reach her wrists, losing balance, as she positions herself to duck under his arms and out of harm's way.

Having our hands in front will set us up for success. Besides physical positioning and visual advantage, this psychologically demonstrates confidence. We who do it feel stronger, and those around us treat us with more respect.

In everyday life, *hands in front* could translate to keeping anything important to us in view. If something matters to you, why leave it out of sight? Yet, I see this all the time. Not paying attention to your money, ignoring the elephant in the room with your partner, avoiding the dentist, or living with years of clutter are common examples. Any of these choices are energetic leaks, because they are always (subtly or not) pulling on your attention.

I think we fear what we'll see if we look at these triggering areas, as if looking at them automatically brings problems. And while seeing things clearly *will* reveal what's not working, we are more likely to correct potential challenges this way. Negativity doesn't like to fester in plain sight. By maintaining awareness of the people and things that matter to you, you'll have the opportunity to address any issues when they are small enough to handle easily.

Literally or figuratively, having your hands in front means you're less likely to get surprised by conflict, or to end up in a situation that you can't handle. Your energetic presence adds to your protection. The more awake you are to your environment, the more prepared you will be for anything and the more harmony you'll live in.

Be Intentional

Living life as a martial art, we must be intentional. Relating with one another in haphazard ways achieves neither victory nor union. Continually asking, "Why am I doing what I'm doing?" increases both vitality and peace. We can ask things like:

Am I aggressive with that person because they remind me of someone who hurt me? Or because they actually deserve it? Am I going to that party because I think I "should," due to FOMO, or because it aligns with my values or goals?

Making intentional choices in life sharpens our aliveness. The equivalent in Aikido practice would be striking at a vital organ such as a kidney, versus scrambling to attack any random spot. Relating mindlessly with life and other people can be reckless. At best, it dulls our energy and dilutes our experiences.

In the dating world, many folks don't know what they want. While it's healthy to meet different people to see who you click with, doing so with no intention can bring heartbreak. Even if you're in a transitional or exploratory time in life, you can be transparent about that. If you ultimately want a life partner or a stable job or home—and are checking out different options to find the best fit—you can own all of it.

In the midst of change, you may be unclear about your intentions. That doesn't make you a bad person, and it doesn't mean you're on the wrong path. In fact, just as a butterfly starts off as a caterpillar in a cocoon, we may need to go through the unknown. However, even in these moments, we can be sure about something. I often ask myself or my clients, "What is one clear next step right now?" Leaning into that certainty and taking that one step will help reveal the next one.

We sometimes have explicit intentions, but they don't seem to match reality. Maybe life circumstances don't seem to support what you want. At these times, I don't advocate dropping your desires. Yet, you must get out of your head and out of black-and-white thinking. You can pray, meditate, or affirm something like this: "I don't know how I'm going to achieve _____, but I'm open to being shown the way. I'm inviting in the resources and support and insights to help me get there." In these cases, you are collaborating with unseen forces, with the Universe itself. This is very Aikido.

Like effective Aikido technique, your specific intentions foster grace in your daily interactions. Vague intentions can lead to injury, on various levels.

Conscious relationships will reveal our habits and unhealed wounds. There is value in commitment, whether it be to a path or a person, because our commitment ensures we'll keep striving to improve ourselves. Without this, we can keep blaming or stay asleep to our unhelpful patterns. But, knowing you're coming back Monday to that same practice partner who bugs you, or that you're coming home tonight to your spouse after that argument this morning—makes it more likely you'll do the work to better your relations.

Having an intention for each of your relationships or activities—and ultimately having intention for your life—makes commitment more approachable. Those who do so usually want to grow. Living this way, does commitment actually become more appealing?

Stop Overextending

If you overcompensate, you never know where your partner actually is. For instance, if you repeatedly initiate plans and your friend or love interest never does, how will you know if they want to see you? And while you may occasionally talk someone out of their bad habits or convince them of things they weren't choosing on their own, how sustainable is this?

I have witnessed many heartaches where one person's hyper-functioning perpetuated both their delusion and the other party's disrespect. While there are exceptions, women are especially prone to this in relationships with men. And anyone who's enabled an addict may relate. We tend to feel shocked when the other person pulls away or falls back into the patterns which we thought they'd outgrown. Oops! Off the mat, disrespect tends to devolve into resentment, withdrawing, and/or attack.

Martially, your unnecessary movement can give your partner an opening he wouldn't have had otherwise. You become ungrounded and easy to take down. And if you want him to act, you'll never give him an invitation to if you keep moving.

Great masters often model the art of non-action. This is another way of saying: You are the center of your experience. Trust this.

How do we not overextend? We must undo the conditioning of living primarily from the head and upper body. We need to root through our feet and move from the inside out, despite the pull of the external world. This is a major leap of faith that supports our empowerment in every way.

During some of my years of intense Aikido study, I was

parenting a small child. When my teacher said, "Your partner should move a lot; you should not," my mind went to the kitchen.

Every time I heard, "Mama, look at this," every time I saw a near-spill or accident, every time she asked for one more thing—I had a choice to run over and do something, or a choice to stay still. Notwithstanding the occasional instance where she had a true need, I learned that holding my ground as a mother commanded more respect. Not only that, but I also had more to give my daughter when I relaxed and conserved my energy. She learned self-responsibility and cooperation more quickly.

Require partner to accommodate you. It should not always be you overreaching. This is neither necessary nor productive.

Of course, relationships should not be one-sided. I'm not advocating narcissism, which is epidemic right now, as the prevalence of loneliness and low self-worth makes for desperate egos. Those who've leaned this way must learn to think of others, and to heal the emptiness they feel inside.

On the Aikido mat, we *take turns* requiring our partner to move more. And in doing so, we discover not only how to defend from our center; we also extend from our own secure position. From here, we can give and give generously.

If you've ever offered more than you had to give, you may relate to the crash and burn that comes next. You likely know well the resentment that follows. There is no room for these things in martial arts practice. Literally, an unstable stance will cause you to fall or get hurt. And these negative emotions will disrupt your capacity to harmonize with your partner. They are best rooted out at the start by your proper positioning.

Don't Feed the Darkness

While we all have negative tendencies and no environment is immune to ego, at least those who enter a dojo are taking measures to improve themselves. And so, it's generally a more conducive place to practice staying on the high road no matter how your partner shows up.

In general, many people are quite unconscious of their own egoic tendencies. In fact, some can be blatantly selfish or mean. How do we handle this negativity?

In my experience, the best bet is to avoid giving the darkness more power. It will take whatever you give it and grow, and then you end up fighting with your own energy as well as it. Whether this means starving out your own unhelpful thoughts or habits, or choosing peace when invited to fight with another, it serves the same goal.

When you meet someone who is out of balance and engage on their terms, you have fed the darkness. This includes defending, arguing, or rushing to put out someone's alleged fire. On the mat, we feed darkness/separation/ego by moving too much, or by moving from an ungrounded place.

We also indulge this negative energy when we stay on the line of attack, versus protecting ourselves by moving our bodies. It's safer to respond by adjusting our position peacefully and quickly. Then, we can better handle it from a place of power, either before it gains—or after it has lost—momentum.

If we see darkness as a black hole to run from at all costs, we are always running on some level and darkness keeps winning. Everything stems from the Divine, and darkness has simply lost its way home. As soon as light touches it, it disappears. Meanwhile, by challenging us, it strengthens and clarifies our light.

When you are provoked, stay centered and move off the line of fire. From there, you can observe from a neutral place, and either mindfully engage or exit.

With certain people in your life, physical contact may or may not be appropriate. Even if you choose not to speak to someone due to their imbalance and its toll on you, there is an energetic conversation happening simply because you notice them. Your awareness offers an invisible light, and even this light brings healing.

The important key—which most of us miss—is to stay disengaged as you notice. You can still love and care for them, yet from this place you will not put yourself in jeopardy. There is a principle of spiritual indifference. Your neutrality is not only your protection, but also their salvation—to whatever level they can accept.

Because you are only able to affect what happens in your space, you must hold your own frequency at truth, love, and light in the face of darkness. In the same regard, we stay centered in Aikido, to ensure that we don't fall over as we throw someone. We cannot allow their aggression or clumsiness to knock us down any more than we should jump into their space to "fix" them.

If I want someone to be more constructive or kind, I will both model that with my actions and also hold the frequency in my energy field. The latter strategy works surprisingly well! Whether they are angry or needy, jealous or appreciative, they can't help but feel what I feel as they put their attention on me. If they're focused on me but can't match my energy, they'll leave! I stay safe and they don't know what's happening, but they change!

On the mat, this is how we transmute any darkness that attacks us, so it must become light. Aikido has this potential to guide us so artfully from a fight to a dance, from destruction to mystic union.

Love Is Fierce

This idea that love is all fluffy like a Hallmark card is a very small part of what it is. In fact, this fluff may not be real love at all.

To me, practicing Aikido means you are a warrior for love. And yet, it involves punching and throwing each other around. Paradoxical? It would be if we were actually hurting each other, but we're not.

Love takes a stand. It won't tolerate you being mean to me, so it shows you where to go. It won't allow me to overcompensate, and so corrects me if I do. Love cares more about the big *you* than it does about the little *you*.

You may identify with your thoughts, feelings, and coping mechanisms—but they are not the true you. A skilled partner will quickly mirror back to you their value (or lack of value). If you do that thing that makes you feel strong, and he resists or withdraws, perhaps love has another way? If you hold back your actual strength and she wilts or butts in, consider again if you have misunderstood love.

Love may be either soft or strong. Love flows in whatever way it must. Too strong or too soft—either way you can inadvertently hurt another. Always being *nice* or trying not to rock the boat is not love.

Compassion will help where there's a true need, but it won't try to protect you from your feelings. It believes you are big enough to handle them.

Aikido will protect your life, but it won't protect your imbalances. Quite the opposite, it will reveal whatever in you is not aligned with love. Love insists on honor, respect, and truth. Love knows who we truly are and will settle for nothing less.

Disrupt to Reconstruct

If both you and your partner are balanced, you can respect-fully observe one another, or you can have a standoff. There may be no real harm here, yet there's not much movement. As soon as—and only when—one person's balance is bro-ken, her partner can take her in a new direction. This art of taking balance is called *kuzushi*. It is a fundamental Aikido principle.

With anyone from your significant other to a co-work-er, there will inevitably come a time where you butt heads or don't see eye to eye. Continuing to push your agenda doesn't work. Sometimes you hit a wall with someone, and you can't so easily get away. The expression "something needs to give" is kuzushi.

It doesn't take much to break someone's balance. My client was wondering how to approach an annual review at work, and I saw they had already planned what to say to her. "Ask them a question," I suggested. This they would not expect. Rather than devaluing herself by defending her requests and needs, she could require they justify *their* comments and decisions. In answering the specific question I recommended, they would have to see and explain how they were honoring her compared to other employees.

To me, this unbalancing is Divine disruption. It may be uncomfortable but it's not actually threatening. We can learn to stay empowered even when we're stretched. And then the moment balance is broken, we unlock the door to something new. The funny thing is there is more security here, not less. This is because kuzushi ensures we have more options.

Both evolution in life and deepening in love require

discomfort. I have seen many a heart crack open before a healthier love appears. Facing those tough issues, acknowledging what's not working, or even taking a break from your boyfriend or girlfriend may be necessary in order to regroup on fertile ground. I have watched how loss and letting go confound us, and then make way for renewed success and creative openings.

On the mat, your throw will fail if you haven't first achieved kuzushi. To try otherwise requires pushing with physical strength alone, and that's not Aikido. It's counterintuitive, but breaking uke's balance is your gift to him. Only when that balance is broken will he experience your technique as a fun ride.

If you are the one whose equilibrium is getting disrupted, try not to resist. Life's curveballs don't go away just because we ignore them. They are there for a reason. We must practice getting comfortable in the discomfort. When we find grace and lightness in the midst of it, then nage (or life) has an easier time taking us to a better place.

Kuzushi is the *tough love* of neutralizing a situation that could otherwise cause harm. Martially speaking, it is a way to minimize the impact of partner's attack. However it occurs, it sends a firm, clear message of "not that, not here—" and yet it does not hurt the other person. It supports her as it surprises her, saying, "Hey, let's try something else!"

Claim Your Space

There are times to be very direct and unapologetic, when you have an obvious need to take care of yourself. And once you claim the space you occupy, defending yourself takes much less work.

On occasion during Aikido training, we require an extra edge to throw an attacker off-balance. This goes beyond our ordinary kuzushi. For instance, if I need to turn my back to him in order to reposition myself, or if I want to enter in more aggressively, I might implement what we call an *atemi*.

An atemi looks like a punch or strike—such as putting your hand in his face. Like all Aikido, its purpose is not to hurt, though it could hurt if your partner does not move appropriately.

From some teachers, I have heard it described in this more-martial sense of "hit him if he doesn't move." On the other hand, some see atemi as more of a positioning tactic. This mindset keeps us out of aggression, while the pose still accomplishes our goal.

Either way, an atemi tells your partner, "Back off! This is my space!" Most of us could use to hone this skill. While it's rarely appropriate in daily life to stick your hand in someone's face, saying "No" or "Stop" is underutilized. We don't need to explain these words, any more than we need to talk through why my hand is in your face if you're physically attacking me.

If I need to assert myself, and conditions don't currently support my doing that, it's time for the "Wait a minute" atemi. If I cannot let things keep going as is, I must break the flow so I can regroup and take care of myself. Beyond not deferring to someone's expectations, this is a strategic (yet honest) curveball I throw.

For instance, maybe you have certain friends or family members that like to run the show. You know they're about to set up the next holiday or party the way they always do, and you don't like it. You can do something to distract and disrupt them before they get too far. "Hey, I made reservations at X restaurant for Friday!" you might say (knowing they always choose a different place). Get creative and stay positive ... but give them an atemi!

Let's say my business partner is used to overriding me and doing everything her way. I could still hold steady and do it my way, in a way that throws her plan off. For this to be artful and not harmful, my intent must be to honor myself and the business, and not to undermine her. But it should make her stop and re-evaluate how she's operating.

One of my clients was getting corrections on his freelance project. While most of the time he accepted the feedback and adjusted his work, the notes he was given recently felt "off" to him. From his well-earned wisdom and confidence, he replied and said, "Thank you, but I won't be changing this part." They took it well! Everyone has an off day sometimes, and just because one person apparently has authority doesn't mean they are always right.

Atemi is an expression of dignity, not disrespect. Self-worth must sometimes take a stand.

The Closer You Are, The Safer You Are

Have you ever avoided someone or something when you were triggered? Made assumptions because you didn't know what was really going on, and then realized things weren't nearly as bad as you thought? Usually, the anxiety we drum up in our minds is way worse than our response to the truth. In general, the more you keep in touch with any important person in your life, you'll be less surprised and more relaxed.

The average Aikido beginner will pull away as a technique is applied to them. Of course, without knowing the proper response, they have reason to resist. A balance of caution (because they aren't sure they know how to keep themselves safe) and willingness (because tightening up can cause further injury) is required here. Much of early training is on how to fall, roll, and respond. It's also about the value of staying attuned to one another.

When we stay close to that person who's leading us into uncharted territory, we benefit from the sensory information they give us. We also benefit from staying close to a changing situation. It's much easier to go somewhere new if we feel it coming.

To our detriment, we tend to yank ourselves away from the unknown in our relationships and lives. As soon as we sense a change, we choose distraction or run and brace ourselves. In doing these things, we make it harder, and it's less likely to go our way.

On the mat, it not only feels better to stay connected to your partner; it's safer. For instance, if their arm comes across your face for a throw, wouldn't you prefer to get hit in the cheek rather than the nose? For this reason, I teach beginners to tuck their nose into their partner's shoulder. It's not instinctive but will make the impact much softer. It also means you'll see more of what they're doing and can therefore preempt potential injury.

When on the receiving end of a wrist lock, we protect our elbows by bending them and we move as we must, even if we feel weaker in doing so. New Aikido students frequently have to unlearn their tendency to lock up here. The pain in remaining tense quickly teaches them.

Psychologically and energetically, your partner will naturally match you. If you punch someone and they apply a technique to control you, they'll be much nicer if you follow their lead. If instead you resist, you provoke them further. Anticipating your next strike, they get meaner. And you enter the game of *an eye for an eye* as union goes out the window.

Do you have someone in your life who's highly reactive or emotional? You cannot directly disagree or provoke them, and it's an art to get them to see your side. This can be agony for straight shooters like myself. It takes a lot of patience, but in these cases, we must slow down to speed up.

Staying close here means acknowledging their point of view. Validate their feelings and empathize, even if you oppose their beliefs. Once they feel seen and heard, they are much more willing to give you what you need.

We can avoid escalated aggression through artful compliance. This means assessing where your risk is greater: in letting go or holding on? At first, we have to practice and think about it. It's not easy at the beginning. In time, it becomes instinct.

True vs. False Safety

Many of us have a skewed sense of safety. We unthinkingly do things that compromise it, while neglecting—even fearing—things that could offer us true safety. We each have specific personal tendencies, due to childhood patterning and other factors, and this can take a lifetime to explore and unravel. That said, I find it helpful to ask this question when I feel stuck or afraid: "Is what I'm doing *actually* making me safer?"

In Aikido training, a classic example is the beginner who muscles through, or who prematurely disconnects from his partner. Both of these choices stem from the fiercely individualistic, competitive mindset that Aikido seeks to rewire.

In day-to-day relationships, we could equate this disconnect with lack of communication, with not sharing our truth, or assuming we know another's without inquiring. It can be scary to authentically communicate, but that doesn't mean silence is safer! In time, a situation can really blow up if needed dialogue has been lacking. Just as entering quickly may diffuse a physical attack more easily, speaking early so as to avoid misunderstanding is a powerful way to "stay safe."

Resistance can show up as arguing, rebelling, or over-powering another without regard for the consequences. It can also show up as overly helping, convincing, or always taking the lead. For others, hiding—or lack of appropriate action—is their chosen safety strategy. Do any of these things work? Maybe temporarily. And while band-aids have their place, core healing undoes the need for a band-aid.

While we may think we get away with them in life,

Aikido swiftly reveals the illusion that these coping strategies make us successful. It challenges us to rethink what true strength is. It beckons us to repattern our knee-jerk tendencies to separate. As we relax into deeper resonance with ourselves and others, we live as a wellspring of life-force which protects us. As we *become* the safe place, our past ideas of protection may prove to be more and more irrelevant.

Turn Towards What Hurts

When we attempt to avoid pain, it gets worse. And our breakthroughs often come with pain. Any woman who's birthed a child naturally can attest to this! Pain implores us to soften; that's what it's designed to do!

I'm not saying we should seek out pain, or that we should refrain from speaking up or changing course when we can. That said, pain is implicit in life. Regretfully, most of us resist making significant changes without it. And so, we'd do well to learn how to handle it when it occurs.

It's common to think that conflict equals pain. You said something I don't agree with and now I'm struggling with what to do. Should I refute your position? Go silent? Respectfully share my opinion? Cut you off? I don't have to suffer. I have these choices and many more.

Depending on the nature of our relationship and the larger picture, various responses may be appropriate. Even when I must completely block someone in order to protect myself or others, it's still costly to repress what I feel. Whatever came up for me with that person will come up again if I don't face it within myself. As I accept and feel my feelings, the tension dissolves and I won't need it repeated. I won't be a match for it in the future.

In some cases, we make things worse when we avoid pain. If I'm people-pleasing so that everyone likes me, I'm struggling inside. If I yank away, fight back, complain, or obsess—I'm perpetuating what I say I don't want.

Staying present and acknowledging the pain will actually protect you better from it. It allows you to get real about it, and to communicate to partner (on or off the mat), "Wow, that really hurt." It urges each of you to do better, to try another way next time. It ensures you won't keep partici- pating in a harmful interaction.

Aikido should never hurt. As soon as we feel that the pressure is enough, or as soon as we see we must acquiesce, we should tap out. When we do, our partners must imme- diately let go.

Certain techniques have the potential for pain, and yet are incredibly beautiful and enjoyable dances when we stay supple. One of these is the *nikkyo* wrist lock, where "letting partner have us" is our best protection. By softening and going along with it, we might even find a reversal here and get out of the situation. Paradoxically, this only works if we relax enough to sense where our opportunities are, instead of gripping for dear life, assuming we're trapped.

To some degree, pain is a state of mind, where we believe we are stuck in a difficult place. We must change this state to change our reality. Adjusting our mindset and rewiring our bodies go hand in hand.

The Value of Sensitivity

You might guess that sensitivity has little place in martial arts, but it's truly the opposite! Besides its role in protecting ourselves from injury as well as fostering harmony, sensitivity also gives us the courage to be strong when strength is appropriate. Only by presence and attunement will we know.

Wishy-washy, tentative movements don't necessarily indicate sensitivity. They're more likely a sign of fear. And the brute strength that gives the masculine a bad rap is not the only kind of strength; in fact, it's frequently a compensation for his misperception of inner weakness.

I believe that acute sensitivity is necessary for the masculine to fully express. Without it, he has no way to gauge whether he's of service or not. This attunement is what transforms strong masculine into Divine masculine. Developing it allows each of us to be more assertive when assertiveness is called for. At times, this energy is the gift that a relationship or community needs.

Assertiveness becomes a problem when someone just has that one channel, and when he doesn't notice when circumstances dictate a softer approach. For instance, charging towards an inexperienced Aikido student with full speed and force is not appropriate. Being extremely bold with someone who's shaky and scared is neither kind nor productive. Not noticing where the other person is at, a mutually supportive encounter is unlikely.

According to the law of karma, what goes around comes around. While this is a Universal law, it also translates literally in the way your partner tends to mirror you. On and off the mat, your well-being improves when you treat others the way you want to be treated. Sadly, by getting hurt we learn what *not* to do, because then we best understand our potential to hurt someone else.

One sign of a skilled Aikidoka is that they sense exactly how hard to throw, based on observing their partner's energy in the moment. Because I have the ability to breakfall or roll safely and quickly, a strong throw feels exciting to me! I am happy when a trained partner feels me and throws me this way! If she's too gentle relative to each of our capacities in the moment, this can also indicate insensitivity.

Sensitivity is not about being *nice*. It's about being aware. It is what fosters a highly dynamic practice or life, as we move smoothly with whatever comes our way.

Writing Practice:
Developing Sensitivity

1. Have you ever learned the hard way that you were being insensitive or that your actions caused harm? Describe what happened and what you learned.

2. Did you ever change course, and become more or less assertive as a result of observing what was needed in the moment? Describe.

3. What are some ways you could cultivate your sensitivity? For instance, you might try meditation or another mindfulness practice, or you could get more curious with loved ones. What ideas do you have?

Be Attuned to Your Openings

I attended an Aikido Halloween party years ago. Dressed as a palm reader, I was reading the palms of many attendees. A highly ranked sensei came over and asked me to read his. And after I did so, he took my palm and kissed it.

My biggest problem here was not our age difference, nor that he was a teacher, and I was a student. While I don't advocate anyone in power taking advantage of those who may rely on them or look up to them, it was something else that really stunned me.

What bothered me most was that I did not give him an invitation to do this. His actions startled me as they came out of the blue; I had not given him an opening. And so, this went counter to everything we learn in Aikido. What kind of master was he?

Good Aikido feels generous even as someone presses into your space, throws you, or makes you run around. Our interactions feel smooth and congruent, because the yang echoes the yin. The openings match the assertions. And so, there is harmony. The attunement between the poles sparks a highly charged dance. Maybe this teacher had had a few drinks, because his Aikido was much different than his party persona.

It felt icky, not enlivening. And I know we have all felt some version of this, where someone treated us carelessly. Because of this, many of us have tended to shut down and hold back. This too, hurts. It hurts those on both sides of what could be a mutually chosen and reciprocal exchange.

Since these types of stories have been highlighted in both recent news and social media, many folks—men especially—have flipped the other way. Good guys don't want to be *that guy*, and so err on the side of not asserting themselves, even in appropriate situations where the openings are obvious. Many women complain to me about this, and the negative results are many. Most notably, women are increasingly over-functioning rather than responding and receiving, opportunities to love are missed, and most everyone is confused.

Beyond this pendulum swing away from masculine assertiveness, apathy is also widespread. More people are zoned out on their phones, immune to their environments. I talked to a single 30-something-year-old who told me she went to bars to meet people, only to find that everyone there was looking at their dating apps versus talking to the people right next to them! In a case like this, invitations to connect are slim to nonexistent.

So no, don't just assert yourself no matter what the other person wants. At the same time, what might happen if you felt for the openings and *went for it* when you received a compelling invitation? How can you offer sincere openings to another?

Who Does the Initiating?

In the past I listened to a dating coach, who recommended that a woman interested in a man should smile and make eye contact with him for six seconds. I tried it once, and the guy definitely got it! This is just one example of how to initiate without overtly making the first move.

Even when we're practicing familiar techniques in Aikido class, our nonverbal invitations to one another are continually present. This becomes even more obvious when new folks join. They don't "do their part," since they haven't learned how to. Because of this, even experienced students can get mixed up about how or when to attack them. This exchange of cues becomes second nature, however, with practice.

From standing in *hanmi* (a triangular stance with one foot in front of the other) to dropping my sword to extending my arm, I invite my partner to strike, in subtle or not-so-subtle ways. Based on which foot I have in front or where my weapon is placed, she has logical choices. If she overrides what I'm offering, Aikido becomes awkward.

I love reminding my students—kids especially—that they're in charge of how things go, even as the other person is punching. A skilled aggressor about to strike will choose the most opportune moment to do so, just as a man may need a few hints or a friendly smile before asking a woman out.

Have you ever had a relationship start one way, and then turn in a completely different direction? Or perhaps you and a family member have vastly different experiences of the same person. Is this because of something *you're* doing? Because of how *you're* being? Probably!

Even in the midst of technique, this play of "who's initiating?" never stops. If I try to block my partner's movement with my hand instead of flowing with him, it's very likely he'll change his technique. He is still directing things, but I made it go that way instead of the other. This is similar to how a river shapes a riverbank, even when it looks like the edges dictates the river's flow.

Last week, it was extremely windy outside our dojo. At the end of class, I had the kids sit very still. "Let your body get heavy, like a rock," I said. When they opened their eyes at the end of our brief meditation, I asked if any of them thought we could get still enough to stop the wind. Most said no, and some of us wondered.

"I don't know if we can slow down the wind with our stillness," I said, "but I do know something. In Aikido, the more you stay calm, the more your partner will be calm." Impressively, they seemed to get this.

One person's aggression or gentleness tends to bring out the equivalent in his partner. If he rushes in, overcome with excitement, he risks either having the time of his life or taking a harder fall than he would have otherwise. Knowing this, though, is like a secret sauce. Nothing is simply *happening to you*. How you approach it influences how it will go. Living with a warrior spirit in love, we are prepared for anything as we also tailor our actions according to our desired outcomes.

We are all riffing off each other in the dance of life. And the good news is, that means you can change your world by adjusting yourself.

The Masculine Leads with Direction

The masculine leads with direction, and he does a disservice to life when he withholds this gift. As mentioned, this must be approached with sensitivity, though sensitivity should not automatically imply gentleness.

I remember getting corrected on this when working with a newer student. She was unsure of the movements, and I matched her hesitation as I brought her to the ground. "What are you doing?" my teacher asked.

I explained that I didn't want to hurt her. He knew I knew the technique very well. "Be clear with her," he said. "She's counting on you to show her where to go." I realized I was confusing her more by being tentative, and I have since worked on this tendency with beginners.

The masculine is the part within each of us that directs energy. When it's your turn to do it, do it with loving strength, knowing that this is helpful to the recipient. Don't hurt them, but don't coddle them either. In fact, I would argue that your clear direction is a sign of respect.

In dating, a man who is clear about his intentions and openly pursues a woman fosters her sense of safety. Him being vague and soft does not necessarily support her. Examples of this are the man who expresses interest but never makes a move, or a man who shows up inconsistently. On the other hand, when a man asks a woman out or makes plans for the two of them, she knows where she stands and can then relax.

Anytime you are in a masculine role, this clear direction is called for. Of course, it's appreciated in romantic relationships. In addition, if you are leading a team at work or teaching a class, those you serve are counting on you to tell them what to do. Healthy masculine energy is not power *over* another. It is, *Hey, I'll take the reins. I feel you and know what you need. Rest assured, you can be yourself and know I've got you.*

The Feminine Leads with Energy

Leading with energy is feminine leadership. Because energy is less tangible, it's often undervalued or disregarded in our culture. Body language, subtle cues, and feelings all fall into this category. Inviting our Aikido partner to attack, and the quality of our responsiveness are also examples of feminine leadership.

On a more esoteric level, the feminine leads through frequency and vibration. There are ways to measure vibration, and yet we generally can't see it with the external eye. That said, most of us can relate to *getting a vibe* off of someone, or of *liking the energy* of a certain place. We feel it—and yet what does it look like? That's a mystery.

The feminine embodies grace and poise. She leads with a love that includes herself and all life. She leads with "Yes, please" and "No, thank you." She sculpts her life based on what feels good and what doesn't feel good. She allows you in if you meet her requirements, and if not, you are spun out of her orbit. Dare not disrespect her, because she can roar and destroy.

When we move our emotions and then our world changes, this is the power of the feminine. Holding a deeply felt intention has impact and tends to sculpt those around us. Similarly, as soon as we think of attacking our Aikido partner, energy follows our thought. Whereas those who are haphazard with their actions and do not put feeling behind them are not nearly as powerful. Masters may artfully disguise their intentions to buy time in order to cultivate more harmony, and never to manipulate for selfish purposes.

In romantic love, it is often the feminine partner who feels first when something is off. It is frequently her who receives a vision of where things could go, before they go there. Just as her womb offers spaciousness to grow new life, she taps into inspiration better when she's *in her flow*, and when she has space beyond the day-to-day demands on her attention. Ideally, her masculine partner will hear her feelings and visions and allow them to inform his direction.

Energy is what embodies action. No arm, no sword has power without energy behind it.

The masculine looks to the feminine for her yes or her no. Direction looks to love's flow to determine where to go. Both the masculine and feminine leadership need each other, and life needs them to get along.

Writing Practice:
How Do You Typically Lead?

1. Do you tend to lead through words, actions, emotions, or energy? Write about your reflections here:

2. Are there ways you could improve your masculine leadership?

3. How might you step into more effective feminine leadership?

Notes

Be Generous

"You're stingy!" my partner sniped and dropped his hands. It was his turn to grab me in *kokyu dosa*, a seated technique where uke grabs both of nage's wrists. *He was the one grabbing, so what did I do wrong, I wondered? Wasn't I just waiting for him?*

I understood once we switched roles, and he extended his arms towards me. It looked as if he was hugging an invisible ball in front of his chest. Rather than taking control of something weak, I had to reach up and contend with his energy to get hold of his wrists. He definitely wasn't just waiting passively for me. Even though I was attacking, he was offering me something.

I ask my Aikido kids if they know what "stingy" means. If not, I explain, "It's when you don't want to share." They get that, and they know it doesn't feel so great.

"Imagine your arms are water hoses full of water," I'll say to them before their partner grabs. "No spaghetti noodles allowed in here!" They laugh and fill their arms with life force, as if they've just blown up a balloon. This simple visual allows them to find the relaxed power based in harnessing ki.

Beyond just a physical exercise, this practice stems from a generous mindset. Spiritually, it comes from the remembrance that you are the universe, you are love itself. Collapsing assumes the opposite—that you're not important, that you're not worthy, and that you've already lost.

Rejection, betrayal, and moments of hurt may lead us to shrink. Aikido philosophy reminds us that this never works. Spacing out on the mat makes us vulnerable to injury. Going numb in life means we have even less influence over what's happening. And then, we tend to absorb whatever's around, which usually means we feel more pain—not less. It almost always backfires.

We all feel deflated at times. How can we stay engaged with life, even when we're hurting? What I know from Aikido is: Don't stop moving, stay present in the here and now, and protect myself while avoiding harm.

It's not about pretending you're excited when you're not, nor is it about opening indiscriminately. At these times, remembering the Aiki-spirit within means you can feel love and revere life no matter what's happening around you. Even in the midst of grief, you can be full and present. You, the infinite being, walks hand in hand with you, the fragile human. You become more fortified when you're challenged, because you must include more. This grows your compassion, and you become a beacon of peace.

Someone who's been hurt may subscribe to the philosophy, "Never let your partner have the upper hand." Not only does this prevent you from feeling deep love, but it also actually limits your ability to *discover* whether you can trust someone. And so, you never get out of the *freeze* pattern, even with new people and even after the hurt is long gone.

If you recognize yourself here and if you'd like to open to new relationships, you could try this: From a balanced stance and giving mindset, ask yourself what you feel able to give. Where are you willing to be vulnerable? Is that in extending an invitation, letting someone know you like them, or showing them the parts of you that you're less proud of?

In one of these ways or one of your own, selectively let another person have the upper hand, and see what they do with it. If you like the result, perhaps give more. If not, you didn't lose anything you really needed. Meanwhile, you learned something valuable, and you can walk away knowing you did your part.

Being able to address adversity safely, in any way needed, is a great confidence-booster. Proactively engaging—not running away—is a muscle that can be developed. And if someone is dangerous, your best bet may be letting him pass or moving yourself out of the line of fire—yet this can be done without fear.

In a committed partnership—which could include anything from your beloved to the person you just bowed to in Aikido class— it's disrespectful to show up limp or empty on an ongoing basis. Barring an occasional period of illness, grief, or exhaustion, it's unfair to expect the other person to bring all the energy. Eventually they'll hit their limit, and the juice will run out for both of you.

Be generous, and also be clear on how you can do that. It's better to fully give something you have plenty of, versus faking it or making yourself give something you're starved for.

Give and you will be given to. Take and you will be taken from. Whether it's your vibration or your actions or both, you'll experience the reciprocal result. I believe this is the reason spiritual traditions recommend tithing, donating a percentage of your income. It may seem counterintuitive to give when you feel depleted, but—approached correctly—it may be the way back to strength.

Choosing to give and steering clear of taking is what distinguishes healthy feminine and masculine versus their all-too-prevalent toxic aspects. For our relationships to be mutually supportive, this is not just a matter of proper manners. Nor is it simply a matter of good technique on the Aikido mat. The spirit of sharing is what perpetuates life.

The good news is that life is already inside us. On our best days and our bad days, this inner spark burns steady. Connecting with others reminds us. This is one reason I feel Aikido is so healing. It pulses us back into communion with nature, ourselves, and each other.

Giving Direction versus Giving Energy

Now that giving has been established, how do you know when to give energy versus when to give direction? Do you need to know?

While the most important thing is to stay on the side of giving rather than taking, there is an art to which type of giving to offer. When two people in a dynamic try to give to each other in the same way, frustration occurs.

Let's say you are a teacher or counselor, doing your best to guide and advise. And then, your student or client tells you how much they know and what they've decided to do. There's very little exchange to be had here!

What if you're really excited to relax at the spa, but there's no receptionist and you don't know your way around? You finally find your massage therapist and she's crying and telling you about her problems. Would you feel held or guided? Would you be able to unwind?

In order for one person to flow, the other has to go. When that calm, loving voice says, "Here's what we're going to do, here's how this is going to go," our nervous systems can unwind.

I have known yoga teachers who love to go to yoga class, not because they cannot practice alone, but because they crave being led for a change. Aikido is similar. It's refreshing to get thrown around, since I spend so much time guiding others.

If I insist it's time to attack on your right side and you insist it's the left, we are both leading from our masculine, and we're in a battle. Alternately, when we each try to follow the other, we flail and cease to practice.

In life, it's a bit more nuanced. Who should pick where

a couple lives, or where the kids go to school, or how the money is handled? What are the processes for getting things done within a company or organization?

To begin to answer these questions, we can at least notice, "Oh, we're butting heads! We're both trying to drive in different directions." Or "We haven't included any empathy or flexibility in our decision-making process. Let's try adding that in." Or "After talking about how everyone feels all day, we haven't gotten anywhere. Let's set some goals and make a plan!"

If no one is taking decisive action, you can request that the other person does, you can increase your feminine leadership and offer the invitation, or you can step forth yourself. Through martial awareness (keenly assessing your surroundings) and inner attunement, the next correct step should reveal.

Simply having the intent to join with life force, I believe, will preemptively solve much of this before it happens. And when there is a clash or dull moment, the Aikido mindset can speed up its resolution.

Stay Curious

Keeping a relationship alive and current is a practice. It will not happen automatically; in fact, most romances grow duller, and most families deepen their routines over time. How can we counter this?

I believe that the opposite is more than possible, but we must cultivate it. When you walk in the door and see that familiar person, what might happen if you pretended you just met? What might you notice anew? Would you show up any differently?

I wonder if this lack of curiosity is one reason so many of us move away from our families. Even as we evolve, they tend to see us as they've previously known us. Our long-term acquaintances, too, tend to view us through the lens of the past. And we experience them in the same light. For those on a path of personal growth, this can feel stifling at best. Not only does it limit the individual, but it also erodes the relationship when we think, "I know this already." In these cases, the one who "knows" is no longer relating with an actual person, but rather with a picture.

In Aikido, they say the most dangerous person is a strong beginner. This person wields an increasing amount of power, with neither the reciprocal wisdom nor the awareness of potential danger. Assuming they know, both they and their training partners are at the mercy of what they *don't* know.

We must remain humble if we are to continue to learn. We must stay present for love to stay fresh. For our relationships to feel good—both to ourselves and our partners—we must guard against the tendency to become overconfident.

In Aikido, there's a notable difference training with that

strong beginner versus someone who's been at it for decades. It's not just about masters taking down bigger guys with more strength. I can often tell someone's expertise by how fluid and easy it is to work with them. There's no "clunk," no struggle. I feel taken care of, and like a high level of exchange is happening.

Whether it's Aikido or love or something else, there is something you excel at. In this area, you're bound to cross paths with many beginners. Here, your challenge is to make life and love more important than winning or being "right." The more we succeed, the more options we have.

With mastery, your choices stem from grace and bring balance. There are times to take care of yourself, realizing that the other person does not know how to. There are moments to move *as if* the other person acted correctly, rather than waiting for them and then getting mad when their ignorance inevitably shows.

At other times, your instincts will tell you not to write someone off. Rather than assuming they don't understand or won't give you what you want, you stay open. Maybe they'll blow you away? It may cost you nothing to get out of the way and see how they show up. It could pay off in ways that surprise, delight, and elevate you.

Keep Your Gaze Soft

Often a new student will ask what to look at in the midst of technique. The best answer I've heard is: "Which part of the sunset do you look at?"

Whenever our eyes lock onto the strike or weapon heading our way, we go into *fight* mentality. Even if our response is *freeze* or *flee*, we have lost Aikido. We have stepped out of our power, and the other person has won.

Have you ever been in an argument, and then suddenly saw the big picture and realized the silliness of your fight? What if your greater goals for yourself and the relationship took precedence over the immediate squabble?

In Aikido we train to remain centered and free, no matter what is happening. Regardless of how an opponent is apparently threatening you—you can manage it as long as your focus is broader than just the attack. By maintaining diffuse awareness of the whole situation, your partner's grab or strike ceases to be the center of your Universe. Yes, it may be coming at you, but as soon as you move in any number of directions, that changes. It's up to you to claim your authority to do so.

The paradox here is that you still need to address the attack. It's just easier if you first protect yourself and keep it in perspective.

When someone in your life is upset or ungrounded, it's common to get swept away by their energy. This is especially likely with those you love or see often. Have you ever found that it went well to join someone like this in their chaos? They might temporarily feel better when you do. They might complain or even punish you if you don't. That said, their higher self will rise when you stay calm. And ultimately, you'll both feel better.

How would it be to walk through life with a balance of full presence and openness? I find it to be protective—not only on the mat and in relationships, but in various arenas such as navigating city streets, playing a sport, parenting, or managing a business.

By keeping a larger focus, we are also more likely to get what we want. How often have you latched on to a certain outcome, person, job, or way of doing things—and then realized there was a much better option if only you'd looked around? Success may not lie in whatever we're staring at; yet it may be right on the periphery, easy to find with a soft gaze.

Choose Rather Than Grasp

There is a subtle distinction between grasping at something and choosing it. We can feel it on the mat, as well as in how someone approaches love, money, or anything they want. And while choosing coexists with ease and success, grasping tends to backfire.

On the surface, it can look almost the same. A newer student, learning a tenshin (drawing) opening, may think he is pulling an opponent to him. Not quite!

Aikido doesn't feel like getting yanked on. Aikido says: *I'll go where you want me, if you inspire me, if it's a direction I was heading anyway.* We cultivate the art of surprising our partner, not being where she expects us to be. Perhaps instead, you duck under her arm and compel her to come find you in your new position, right where you want her. From here, you join and move together on your terms, without forcing anything.

Besides beginners, certain individuals are more prone to grasping. For example, a student with a fiery temperament may exhibit natural talent with quick, decisive movements. That same person can also be jerky, grabby, and overextended. When I see this theme, I'll suggest practicing more like water, less like lightning. I have seen these folks transform in a way that keeps their speed and precision—yet in a more stable, flowing manner.

Some folks have trouble letting go—on or off the mat—and so they must reprogram *holding on at all costs* as their default setting. Others hit discomfort when they hold on, and those are the people who need to practice staying connected.

Beyond the technical aspects of positioning and timing,

the art of choosing exists within a different mindset as compared to grasping. Grasping feels bad to everyone involved,
because it's based in misperception. Grasping says, *I'm not
powerful. I can't have unless I do. Getting what I want has to be
hard. You and I are in conflict.*

Choosing knows that no matter what's happening *out
there*, the power of love is inside of me. Only by committing
to that—owning it 100% without any hesitation—do I per-
suade the energies coming my way to align with love.

100% Commitment to Love

You're either 100% committed to love, or you're not. Remembering that love is not people-pleasing, and in fact has a wide range of expression, makes this easier. Love might show up as:

- "Since I'm prioritizing X right now, I won't be available for Y."
- "I'm willing to be assertive."
- "Because I feel strong, I am comfortable to surrender."

Being "all in" with love can be challenging in life, so I find it helpful to practice on the Aikido mat. This gives us a framework, a mindset, and a body memory of how to do it. We can draw from this remembrance when a life partner, boss, or family member pushes our buttons.

The question, "What would love do?" is answered for us in Aikido's pure expression. Watching a masterful teacher, it looks obvious. Love holds on when ego wants to let go, love redirects rather than agitates, and love engages in a way that invites goodwill—even in the face of aggression or the unexpected.

How often have you asked, "What would love do?" when confounded in life? I suggest asking yourself this question when you're feeling stuck. I recommend it when you're unsure how to act, or if you're wondering whether to speak up about something. And, if you keep doing the same things but still aren't liking the result, ask, "What would love do?" and see if another approach comes to mind.

Choosing love, in the bigger sense of love, is an antidote

for shame or guilt. It takes us out of greed or lack or competition, and it frees us from stagnation.

If we think "I'm good if I love and I'm bad if I don't love, and this is what love is supposed to look like," we just missed love! We may judge others in a similar fashion, and yet we rarely find love when we're coming from this type of place.

Love is simple and easy if we allow it. It's about dropping pretenses, recognizing what we already are, and choosing not to do all the things that counter this.

Would you like to try committing to love 100%? While this may be a lofty goal, it's worth striving for. We are all going to mess up at times, and so letting it be simple will help. If you just commit to coming back to love each time you go off track, you'll gain traction in this process. A little amusement really helps. And please remember that love includes yourself.

Surprisingly, I find that going all in with love can be easier when the stakes are higher. When you're about to get punched if you don't blend, you'll do it. If someone keeps draining you financially or energetically and you haven't stood up for yourself, you learn to love yourself pretty darn quick. And after enough heartbreak and loneliness, you say, "enough already," and open yourself to new friends or romantic prospects.

Hopefully we don't have to get to the breaking point before we choose love. On a collective level, this shift may seem long overdue. Fortunately, there is a ripple effect. And the more we each say 100% YES to love, the more we contribute to healing the world beyond our sphere.

The Game of Manipulation versus the Art of Love

It's a fine line between the game of manipulation and the art of love. While externally the two might look the same, they differ—both in how they feel, and in the assumptions underlying either stance.

Manipulation takes something I think I need because I believe I don't have. The dance of love says, "Let's play together to increase our joy and creativity, because we both have."

Manipulation gives in order to get. Love gives in order to share and grow. We can love cleanly and exuberantly, as soon as we realize what we're made of.

Few of us were raised completely free of scarcity mentality. Perhaps there was plenty of money, but a shortage of attention. Even in the most nurturing of environments, a health issue or family crisis may have provoked a sense of lack.

No one is immune to feeling this at times, because contraction is implicit in expansion. Limitations propel personal growth, yet they should not be confused with lack.

Whatever type of scarcity we've experienced, it takes some rewiring to choose otherwise. Not only must we learn not to manipulate, but there is also an art to effectively relating with others who do. Whichever side of the coin you're on, it's not about shame or blame. It's about aligning your stance with love based in giving and having.

For example, in resisting someone who gives in order to get, you tend to end up in a push-pull dynamic. You can make them wrong, stew in frustration, or find another way. Just as you would treat a beginner in Aikido class, consider that they don't know better. Then, you are free to choose as love would. Perhaps disengage, or just move in whatever way you would if things were going well.

One common way people manipulate is through chaos. Have you known someone like this? They don't do what they say, they keep changing their story, or they're nice one day and a monster the next. One might argue that they aren't purposely trying to control. Could it be that they feel so much lack inside, that they don't know how else to find energy? What if they're just unstable, and unaware of how it spills over? Perhaps they desperately, yet unconsciously, seek control because they feel so dysregulated inside. In any case, the result is the same. Because you never know what to expect with people like this, you're always under their thumb.

In Aikido, you *must* manipulate an attacker, to get him on the ground and away from you. Yet, maneuvering someone off-balance to protect yourself is not the same as conniving to cause harm, stealing something from another, or ruthlessly attempting to "win" while they "lose."

To manipulate for love's sake, you have to start from a balanced stance. You must be in integrity—meaning, don't be a crazy-maker. If you begin stepping right and then veer left, it undermines your partner's equilibrium. This is also true if you start to attack (or offer your energy) and then change your mind. Once you make a commitment, stay with your partner through the process. Then, they'll more willingly go where you take them.

Being *off-balance* can also show up as rushing, hesitating too much, overly correcting your partner, succumbing to distraction instead of staying present, or throwing someone in a way she's not ready for. Off the mat, the same principles apply.

You will not be controlling through chaos if you do your best to keep your word, follow through with your actions, and remain humble and honest. Attending to your personal growth and to whatever keeps you centered will help. Without doing so, manipulation (yours or someone else's) tends to creep in, since you're running on empty.

The art of love does the thing that takes a 250-pound challenger down with little effort. The art of Aikido takes him where he's not. If a guy like this was pushing straight into me, I could turn my hips and open up the space where I was, letting him fall right into it as I go unscathed. Or I could slide to the side and, from a new angle that didn't argue with his, send him backwards where he has no balance.

If someone in your life is stuck, even if they think *you* are the problem, you don't have to invest in their war. A step beyond self-protection is to show them a higher way. If they are stuck, they are suffering. It's not about your being *right*, although you may be. By not complying and—better yet—inviting them to a place that's off their radar, you exhibit the art of love. Outside the realm of any conflict, there are infinite opportunities.

Has someone ever done this for you? Besides a romantic partner, you may have received this gift from a teacher, a professional advisor, a friend, or a family member. Whoever has the most Divine idea may appear to manipulate the other, but their intent is pure. It's just that we are sometimes so sure of our flawed position, we won't go directly to what's good for us. We have to take the circuitous route.

I remember a story told by a man I knew and his wife. He was having a heart attack but didn't know it. A highly sought-after energy healer, he believed he could cure the pain in his chest with what he knew—energy work. After witnessing this until her intuition told her to redirect him, his wife stepped in. "Remember you have a meeting this afternoon. It's time to go," she said. So, he got in the car with her, and then she said, "Let's just swing by the hospital on our way and check this out." Was this manipulation? Maybe, but it saved his life. Her art of love was bigger than his ego personality in that instance.

More commonly, one person doesn't realize that they leave a mess of the dishes, or talk rudely about others, or sabotage their success by habitually showing up late. Anyone close who is *not* stuck in the same way can apply the art of love to show them what they're not seeing, to everyone's benefit.

Ideally, we exchange roles and do this for one another. Your gifts may not be the same as your partner's, and that's ok. But if you are *always* talking the same addict into sobriety, and your cup has run empty, this is not the art of love. Conversely, holding back what you can easily give cements the numbness so common in relationships. And you're not doing anyone any favors always holding strong, assuming no one has anything to offer you.

Aikido finds the equilibrium between giving and receiving. We don't have to think about it. It's what happens when life overflows from within us.

Bring an inquisitive, cooperative attitude to all your relationships. Do your best to act in ways that are loving to them *and* you. Much human interaction is transactional, where two people perpetually take from each other because they've forgotten who they already are. Even when we care about each other and even on the path of self-growth, it's rare to achieve 100% perfection. Most of us have some shadowy places where unconscious exploitation slips in. Aikido seeks to change this, and it's one of my wishes through this book, to offer another way.

Disappear So They Find You

I have heard many times in Aikido class: "Disappear, so your partner comes to find you." I love this! And thinking about implications off the mat, I realize that this suggestion may sound like game-playing, which I don't recommend.

What I do suggest is to have so much security inside, that you feel ok letting go of partner for a bit. Try to foster such a sense of safety in your partner that they, too, find comfort in the spaciousness. Like breath, like the tides, a timely moment of *nothing* allows the unfolding of *something*.

Unfortunately, many of us struggle to feel this secure, and so narcissistic game-playing is quite common. A person who tends this way relies on the *supply* of energy they get from others. Disappearing on some level is a way to ensure this supply, because it pulls in energy from the one wondering, "Where'd you go?"

On quick glance, these dynamics might look similar to the healthy ebb and flow I just described, yet they are fundamentally different. Let's compare:

The classic narcissistic relational pattern includes four notable stages: *love bomb–devalue–discard–hoover*. Typically, they start with the narcissist offering tons of attention to get the love object excited, then becoming mean or inconsistent to unbalance their target before rejecting them and finally pulling away. The one who got love-bombed wants more of that initial euphoria, and they feel blindsided by what happened. They become increasingly anxious because that special someone disappeared. And so, the rejected one tends to chase. Even when this chasing consists solely of mental and emotional obsession without action, the narcissist takes energy from the person they ghosted. They selfishly use that energy without giving credit or attention to the one who gave it. And inevitably, as their supply dwindles, they circle back to hoover (vacuum) that person in again.

Any of us who've experienced this can relate to the utter confusion it generates. It can be hard to shake these folks, even when we know the relationship is not healthy, because we want to make sense of something that makes no sense. No matter how good it feels when it's good, we must create boundaries and heal our part in allowing it.

In Aikido training, our disappearing strategy also invites partner to chase us. It draws their energy to us, or it manipulates them by sending them somewhere they weren't planning to go. For example, my partner may move to grab my wrists from behind. Noticing this, I reposition my body and hands, so they are not where he thought they were. He has to run around and by the time he grabs, he is already off-center, making my technique easy. That said, I am not doing harm. There's no unwelcome coercion. We just have more fun and get a better workout.

If my partner comes in with an overhead strike, I can reach my arm up to meet hers, then step under her arm and apply my technique from a new angle. It's like I found an open door and walked through. Naturally, she'll come looking to find me, since we were just in the middle of an exchange. As with the prior examples, I am not abandoning my partner here, nor am I forcing anything. Once she started attacking me, she indicated she wanted to connect. Her job is to keep trying, as long as she can comfortably do so. My disappearing is more like a kids' game of hide and seek than it is a narcissistic discard. The key here is conscious, mutual agreement. And the end result is that more energy gets generated for *both* my partner and me, not just one of us.

At every crossroads, no matter what role you're playing, it rarely serves love to provoke your partner. As long as you refrain from doing so, they'll feel comfortable and stay close—even when you surprise them or disappear. Because of your seamless connection, you can afford these disruptions, and in fact use them to generate more love together.

On the mat, this tactic is sometimes described as giving the person attacking a false sense of security. For example, you keep her moving just to take her down when she least expects it. And yes, it is *false* if her only goal is to attack and never fall. From the perspective of conscious love and polarity, one person's receiving is another person's giving. If no one gives in, there is no Aikido, and love goes stale.

In daily life, while some personalities could benefit from being more honest and direct, some of us err too much on the side of *truth at all costs*. We show our whole hand and wonder why we always lose the game. We long for more play, more surprise, and less struggle. To this end, all the truth is not necessary to share all the time. Without some mystery, relationships can go stale. At the extreme, too much truth may even be harmful.

Asking, "What would love do?" I have learned that sometimes less is more. Nothing *can* be more generous than something. Knowing when to keep the peace and take the high road can go a long way in building up love, trust, and safety. You can then lean into that, when the unavoidable conflict eventually arrives.

From a martial standpoint, we do need to change things up when situations aren't working. To counter an attack, disappearing is one strategy. The conditions must support it, though, if we are to use it to switch on love's flow versus shut it down.

Allow for *Nothing* to Find *Something*

Many of my clients struggle with energetic boundaries. No wonder—most of us weren't taught about this in school! Is it healthy to think about someone all the time, to feel what they feel, or to finish each other's sentences? It may temporarily be alluring, but what about 10 years later? What about with someone you're not sure about? Is the excitement still justified, if it distracts you from your own priorities or well-being?

Feeling another person goes better when you feel them as well as yourself, not instead of yourself. It works best when you know whose stuff is whose. And learning to distinguish your own energy from someone else's takes practice. Especially in close relationships, and with family or long-term partners, this can be highly challenging. In addition, giving a well-adjusted person your energy 24/7, even when you're not together, can confuse or demagnetize them.

So often, I will help a client clear someone else's energy out of their field, and immediately that person calls or texts them. It has even happened mid-session! Our connections with others go beyond the body, and people feel it when things change, even if they aren't conscious of it. Withdrawing your energy from a loved one creates a magnet, likely drawing them in.

Too much of this feels empty and cold, and too little of it becomes enmeshment or mucky confusion. With each relationship, day, and season, we have to find the sweet spot.

Giving someone all your attention in early dating will likely repel them. Whereas, keeping a certain amount of tension and mystery can keep the spark alive. In the midst of an important business meeting or family vacation, pulling away would not be in order. Observe what each moment calls for. If you feel you're giving more than you're receiving in a specific arena, then give less. Letting go for a bit does not mean that a relationship is over. In fact, the opposite may be true.

In Aikido, we talk about joining our energies as essential to proper training. So, what happens if you lose hold for a moment? Can you still do something? Yes! You can when: 1) you regain connection before your partner changes course, and 2) you stay smooth, and refrain from instigating conflict.

Good Aikido—and the dance of love—necessitates that we accept occasional moments of no control. Reacting at these times only slows down—and may even prevent—our recovery. What if we instead enjoy these unexpected offerings of freedom, asking "I wonder what will come of this?" To prevail, we must stay open and fluid, playing with the magnetism which sparks each next interaction.

On the Aikido mat, sometimes success looks like giving up on what you were trying to do, and then switching to something else entirely. We have an aspect of practice called *henka waza* (where you change midstream to a new technique), as well as *kaeshi waza* (where your partner reverses your technique, and you change roles). I will explore each of these, and their parallels with life, in later chapters.

There is also a fine line between disconnecting and losing it, and intentionally disappearing as an invitation to your partner. The key is to let go of control *when you're already connected*, rather than freaking out and wielding your will after you've lost touch with each other. For instance, a couple that's been married for 20 years might enjoy taking separate vacations. Time for husband and wife to each fill their own cup could re-energize the marriage.

Pursuing someone who's distanced from you rarely goes well, especially when you're feeling lost and ungrounded. If you're not rooted in your own center, find it first before attempting to connect with another. Someone checked out is rarely as attractive as someone warm and embodied. Don't make the mistake of making another person your source, as it will never work that way. Instead, find it within.

If it's you that's pulled away and things feel too far gone, now is not the moment to disappear. Like the tide, like the breath, too much *out* is no better than too much *in*. Draw close again. Enter in, close the gap.

After you regain musubi (connection), a disappearing moment will likely show up in your future. By then, you'll be all the more prepared to sail through it with flying colors. Perhaps your comfort zone will have shifted, to realize that healthy relationships are often infused with some extra space.

Strong Grip, Loose Everything Else

I have made many a mistake where I was too soft on the outside, and yet charged with anger or fear on the inside. Once I remember asking for what I wanted while believing I couldn't have it, fearing failure and rejection, and fighting an imagined enemy in my mind. Guess what? I didn't get what I wanted!

Fortunately, I saw what I had done in retrospect, and I asked the other person for a do-over. Months later, I shared from my heart the gist of what I'd wanted to say the first time. I owned the unhelpful defensiveness I'd brought to our earlier conversation. This felt much better, and it restored the sweetness between us.

When we grab someone in Aikido, we don't want to be externally wimpy while filled with internal tension. On the contrary, it is advised to have a solid grip, and to be supple otherwise. Besides the kindness and respect implicit here, this is for many reasons:

For one, your relaxation makes it harder for the other person to feel your center. Therefore, they have trouble breaking your balance. You are giving them something to work with, but you aren't giving yourself away by giving them everything you've got. You maintain self-respect by not putting yourself in jeopardy.

Second, being pliable is safer for you. So is keeping your grip firm. This ensures that you'll feel where they're going and respond skillfully, thereby protecting yourself. It means your landing will be softer if you do go down. There's rarely a reason to get all worked up; your ease will serve most encounters so much more!

Third, you give the other person a healthy challenge, to

truly feel and then influence you. Neither muscular force nor mechanical movements will work for them. Once they have you, your flexible body and clear grip are what allow them to practice effectively. In this way, you avoid enabling other people's bad habits. You become a healer and a teacher just by being.

When you are simultaneously clear and calm, those you touch tend to feel reassured and uplifted. Whereas, asserting yourself forcefully increases the likelihood you'll either instigate a fight or send someone running. If you're obsessing over a goal, and you're high-strung and anxious around getting what you want, it almost doesn't matter how you show up. Your energy will work to repel your desire, even if you think you're doing everything perfectly.

Here, your energy broadcast says, "I need to win, convince, and get approval—or I'm not ok." It screams, "I'm not safe, so I have to overcompensate before he hurts me!" These emotional states are human, yet they don't improve relationships. When we feel them, it's time to breathe, slow down, and rediscover our own foundation.

Our underlying assumptions and how they express are rarely conscious. And once we see what's going on, it takes time to both overcome our negative emotions and teach the body new patterns. I can't count how many times I've made a mental decision or had a spiritual epiphany, but flailed when it came to actually doing what I knew was best. One of the reasons I love Aikido is because the physical realm is the slowest to change. Perhaps we can speed up our personal evolution by heading straight to our somatic patterns?

Aikido is not only about defending ourselves against others. Implicit in our practice is the realization that we experience others based on what we offer.

When you want something in life, what if you could ask, invite, assert, decide, AND be detached about the outcome? The ask is your strong grip. Your detachment is the surrender that fosters safety, connection, and creative possibility.

Writing Practice:
How Are You with Asserting Yourself?

Have you ever been too hesitant in asserting yourself? This could look like: saying what you think and then apologizing for it, withholding your truth when it would benefit a situation to share it, not showing up for someone or something you truly care about, being inconsistent with your actions, or being unclear in offering an invitation.

1. If you said "yes" to any of the above, how did it go? How did it feel?

2. Has anyone ever showed up in these ways with you? If so, how was that experience?

Relaxation = More Power

We were working with *jo*, a wooden staff, at one of our Aikido winter camps in Florida. The sensei demonstrated how the more of the jo we held, the more control we had. However, he explained that holding less of the jo gave our movements more power. In the latter case, we relaxed more, and the weapon swung more freely.

The truth in these concepts echoed far beyond my Aikido practice. I gazed out at the ocean, reflecting on the continual interplay of power and control in my life.

I know well the appeal of control. When I think I know what's happening, I believe I won't be hurt. At times I go for a familiar comfort, rather than chancing disappointment with something that might end up light years better. I don't read the menu. I don't look around to see who else is at the party. I avoid telling you what I really feel. I keep picking the same types.

Therse's nothing wrong with enjoying your favorite latte or hanging out with your BFF, oblivious to the other people or options. You and your spouse may love your Friday night routine or your annual family vacation to a certain spot. Fast forward a few years without variation, how interesting is this life?

On the other hand, have you ever felt the joy in spontaneously going somewhere that you've always wanted to go, but never took the leap? Can you think of a time you had a breakthrough, once you finally risked sharing something vulnerable with someone important? Do you recall ever testing out a new way of responding to that chronic conflict, and feeling simultaneously more alive and closer to another as a result? I know I have!

In the latter examples, relaxation feeds power. Not needing things to be a certain way, you open the door to greater potential. You unlock dormant life force.

Excitement has a place, and so does security. In both the practice of Aikido and the dance of love, we cannot relax when our foundation is shaky. We shouldn't try. When your stability is compromised, that is not the moment to let go of control. In spiritual circles, some judge security and favor "letting go" to a fault. My lived experience has shown me that we open more when our foundation is strong.

To ensure safety, you'd firmly hold the base of a sword, so that it doesn't fly away as you cut. To express yourself freely, you'd need to feel safe with whomever you're speaking with. Why do you think we act out most with those we feel will not leave?

If I'm sick and I know that chicken soup will make me feel better, is that the day to order the chef's latest experiment? Maybe not. I need to re-establish my well-being in times like this. If I'm depleted and you want to have a big conversation, I'd serve us both better if I get some rest and show up for you resourced. At certain times, control might be the most valuable thing to find. And once that's established, a generous dose of relaxation boosts relational immunity.

Changing Course

Aikido never stops. It keeps uniting, unbalancing, and uniting again. While everyday classes ask us to demonstrate prescribed movements, I love to cut loose in freestyle practice. Called *jiyu waza*, this practice reveals what our bodies know and calls forth our instincts. It demands we stop over-strategizing. We must leave room for the unexpected here—without sacrificing confidence or commitment.

I have prepared and watched others prepare for black belt tests, where a common mistake is made with henka waza. In henka waza, we start executing one technique and then change to a different one. Getting ahead of ourselves and planning what we're going to do next, it's easy to rush to the second technique before really attempting the first one.

Budo, the martial way, is based in bravery. It insists we fully show up for whatever is in front of us. No running. No flopping around and pretending to be here so we can get there. It is not in the future, anticipating what's to come. It is right here, right now.

After hearing my sensei sternly correct this mistake in both me and others, I get it. Aikido teaches us to live fully, and to sharpen our edges. Tomorrow will have so much more meaning when we embrace today. Without doing so, we can change lovers or jobs or homes over and over, and yet remain in the same spin cycles.

Have you ever been through a rough breakup, a health crisis, or some trying time—and found so much more appreciation on the other side? Our rewards taste sweeter when they follow these bitters. While I never would have chosen some of my challenges, and have prayed I could hurry them up, hindsight has shown me their purpose. Navigating the stress made me into the person I am today, and I wouldn't have otherwise been ready for more fortunate times that followed. We don't always get to skip ahead.

It's not just the bad that paves way for the good. Savoring quality time with loved ones, or taking holidays or weekends to reset, will also fortify us for a busy work week or time apart. The more we can truly recharge, the more energy we will have for our future demands.

In my work as an intuitive healer, my clients sometimes ask me, "What's going to happen?" Though it may seem paradoxical, the more honed I become in my craft, the less I will answer these types of questions. And that's because it's rarely productive to look ahead! Ninety+ percent of the time, there is something that needs attention right now, that the client doesn't want to look at. It may be in her blind spot, and that's ok. That's why she called me.

I love to help people get to their best possible future. And, knowing too much about where we're headed can actually undermine that. We create based on what we focus on, and we are all quite impressionable. A love warrior fares better in facing the uncomfortable mystery, than she does in preconceiving an outcome she doesn't prefer. This is a moment where relaxation wins out over seeking control.

All we can know is present time. We may think we are going one way, and we need to think this in order to end up positioned for where we are *actually* going. For instance, you may have felt drawn to explore a romance with someone, only to learn another important lesson. You may need to think you're breaking up with your lover, so that you each can shift enough to make your relationship work. Real-life henka waza could look like moving or changing jobs, not for the long term, but simply because you needed to meet someone who became fundamental to your path elsewhere. This becomes amusing after it has pissed us off enough times. We learn to surrender and stay attuned, once resistance and righteousness have proven pointless.

Let's say my client isn't sure where she stands with her boyfriend. He did something she didn't like, and she has needs he's not meeting, but she's not speaking up. Jumping to, "Is he going to leave me? Is this how it's going to be? Am I ever going to get what I want? When will this change?" is totally human. I've been there, asking everyone but the person himself. But there is a more empowering choice: face the feelings and walk through the experience.

What she doesn't see may be how *she* is showing up. Would her boyfriend change if she unraveled her reactions and neediness, and replaced them with steady responsiveness? What if her inner child is screaming for healing by recreating a pattern from age seven? Perhaps her man's transgression is innocent and minor, but all she can see is that 7-year-old's immense pain. Giving herself space to heal inside could create a new future.

Best case, she could share her truth with him and totally transform the dynamic. Being invited to provide for her and witnessing her authenticity could magnetize him in a way that her stewing and withholding never did. It's also possible that her willingness to admit what's not working might give her the clarity she needs to change course. Maybe he is a jerk. He may not honor her or be a fit for her. Yet by showing up for herself, she moves to the next thing standing tall, feeling worthy and alive. If tears fall, they are able to fully release. Unkinked, she opens her door to joy.

Life is not as hard as we make it. Love is the most

natural thing to be, share, and have. Do what makes sense based on what is in front of you, and trust that the next step will appear. Connection is always pulsing and wanting to be found, so keep feeling for it. Take your time and don't give up.

Reversing Roles

Many spiritual teachings emphasize the importance of continual awareness. Darkness or negativity slip in more easily when we are distracted. Paying attention protects us energetically, mentally, emotionally, and physically.

Within advanced Aikido training, we sometimes find the potential to reverse roles and throw the partner who was just throwing us. Called *kaeshi waza*, this practice tests the attacker to keep finding his ground and center. Only by maintaining this will he recognize and seize the moment to thwart his partner's attempted throw. Paradoxically, his flexibility also increases his chances of taking control. The key is not to clue his partner in to where he is going. He should not let on that anything is amiss. He should play along and then boom—switch it up when she least expects it.

Now, she can only avoid reversal when she avoids distraction. In addition to paying close attention to what's happening, her movements must be precise and well-connected. She cannot fake it. Here, any sloppy, habitual movements come back to bite her. She must be honest and clear with her position and timing. Kaeshi waza makes us face what is actually happening in the moment, not what we imagine is happening.

Off the mat, kaeshi waza might equate to a betrayal, or a thwarting of your expectations. It goes like this: *I thought X was happening and I got Y. How can this be!?*

It can be when you're inattentive, when you leave a gap in the connection with your partner. This is where one spouse cheats after years of neglect. It happens if you don't talk through your expectations in dating. If I think we're in a monogamous commitment and you're just enjoying your summer while seeing different people, we have a problem. Or at least, I don't have the assurance I thought I had.

Over the last two decades, I've worked with many folks who felt deceived by a significant other. In extreme examples, he had a secret wife and family in another town, or an addiction or other serious problem. Something more subtle, yet highly impactful, is the potential for relational upset caused by the interplay of energy between two people. What I see a lot is the woman (usually)—or more anxious partner—overextending her energy and then feeling shocked when he pulls away or isn't on board the way she thought he was.

In Aikido, partner can reverse our technique and take control if one of three things happen. Interestingly, these same three behaviors can contribute to experiences of betrayal in life. Here's what they are:

1. *We force things* or push with muscle strength and are not sensitive to our partner. Not feeling what's happening with the other person, we can neither truly relate with them nor do effective Aikido. That gives them the opening to throw us instead.

2. *We aren't centered* with our stance and energy. We aren't in alignment or have compromised our integrity in our body. Our lack of integrity makes us weaker and easy to push over. While it can be tempting to bend for the other person, we have more power in holding steady within ourselves.

3. *We disconnect* from the relationship or have blind spots. Pulling away from conflict or getting distracted, why should we be surprised if they do something we didn't see coming?

A few years ago, I experienced three major betrayals all at once, in three different areas of life. As intense as this felt, in retrospect I see how empowering this season turned out to be. While each situation had its own circumstances and cycle, here is how the worst of the three played out:

Initially stunned, it took months to wade through the grief and shock, and to start picking myself up again. Following that, anger erupted as I processed what the other person had done. I felt like I was really starting to understand what happened, and yet so much focus was on *him*. Realizing I needed to reclaim my energy, I disciplined myself to take *no contact* a step further. Refraining from communicating or looking at his social media was not enough, because I still felt psychically entwined. Once I realized this was not working for me, I used my meditations, affirmations, prayer, and everything I could to redirect my attention back to me and my chosen life. By then, almost a year had passed. And finally, I started to get some real a-has (not just concepts) about my part in how the betrayal had happened.

The concept of kaeshi waza forces us to face up to our own participation in situations we don't like. What I realized was that prior to these three betrayals, I had made the same three mistakes that would allow a partner to reverse my technique on the mat:

First, I wanted it my way. It's not that I was insensitive; I simply didn't allow myself to inquire or truly see where the other person or group was coming from. To do so would have revealed our different needs or realities, and I falsely believed I could brush past this part. I was attached. I thought my vision was good in each case, and maybe it was. However, more needed to be considered if I was to either co-create with these particular people or exit consciously before they left me abruptly. If differences are too great, sometimes relationships or groups need to break up, and this was the case with two of my three betrayals. Thankfully, the other one resolved once we were able to really sit down and hear one another.

I also realized that, prior to being betrayed, I had compromised my own integrity. In the same way I might give up my center during Aikido practice, my actions weren't unified with *all* of me. This went beyond the occasional compromise needed for long-term relationship. I kept investing and hoping my fulfillment was right around the corner, even though my expressed dealbreakers were not met. I habitually over-gave, not just once in a while, and definitely more than the other person did. Making excuses for his hard times, I justified these things even though they felt bad inside. I waited too long to speak up about certain unfulfilling dynamics, and I acted unnaturally the longer I withheld my truth.

While Aikido 101 teaches us to stay connected, I realized I had not been *close enough* to certain situations to maintain a healthy influence on them. And just as physical conflict can scare us into pulling away on the mat, these high-stake relationships—and the fear of messing them up—activated some *flight* tendencies within me. Sadly, my avoidance was one ingredient in the betrayal, but I didn't see that until I was on the ground.

Find Where Your Partner Is Not

Once you initially blend and protect yourself from potential conflict, how do you make sure the source of the conflict is neutralized? When faced with a human attacker in Aikido class, we learn to *find where our partner is not*. Literally, we take her where she has no energy.

From a competitive mindset, we tend to push into someone's body in attempt to defend ourselves. And sure—knowing where my partner is, I can certainly apply effort and fight. Knowing where he's *not*, something more magical happens. I discover an opportunity to easily compel him off course. Aikido occurs here, where I influence him without a battle.

This principle is implicit in why we seek relationship. We *want* to be taken where we're not! Just because we forget this in challenging times doesn't mean it's not true. The beauty in partnership is that it makes us bigger. It inspires our heart, mind, and soul beyond our prior constricts. Good relationships heal us.

As an intuitive healer, I heal by simply being neutral where my client is not. Connecting with me allows them to feel the fresh perspective I have—and then they cannot stay stuck. Sure, I have techniques just like I do in Aikido practice. But the real juice is the energy transmission.

From a technical perspective, you can easily knock someone down by sending her where she has no legs. Imagine a three-legged stool and project her where her third leg would be but isn't. If instead, you push into your partner's structure, don't be surprised if she feels like a brick wall. Have you ever had this kind of futile standoff with someone in your life?

As the holidays approached, one woman did not want to see her in-laws. She felt both a compulsion to take her family somewhere else, and a charged resistance as she rehearsed an agonizing future scene involving her in-law's encroachment. Those two possibilities were her two legs, so to speak. If her husband tried to convince her of one and if she got to defending the other, they'd just see-saw back and forth.

Despite the seemingly unsolvable tension here, he could take her in a new direction and support all parties by suggesting another option, something she hadn't thought of. Maybe she could go on her own little trip, while his parents visited the rest of her family? What if changing the location or the guest list felt different? In any case, she just needed a renewed outlook to help her feel uncaged.

Sometimes, the *line of attack* is within one person. We antagonize ourselves with doomsday scenarios, feared boogeymen, or punishing thoughts of being trapped. It's possible to self-reflect and adjust this, but we may require help. Just as a physical throw could reroute our body into an exhilarating roll, simply talking to someone who sees beyond our black-and-white ideas can bring tremendous relief.

On and off the mat, you can only find where your partner is not *when you are relaxed*. The tighter you are, the less you feel. If the husband above attempted to prove the good intentions of his parents at the expense of other perspectives, solutions would seem impossible. In the heat of conflict, Aikido trains us to feel for the openings, where the potency of our ki (energy) can work around brute force.

Feeling where someone is not, you not only join your energy with theirs. In fact, you remind them of the unity they already have with the Universe. You move them out of stalemate. You invite infinite flow to erupt out of an apparent void.

Just as we all benefit from getting off our two legs at times, we each have the regular opportunity to lead others where they need to go. Do not underestimate your capacity to open up someone's world when you stand surely and lovingly on a different line. Ultimately, we are all seeking expansion, and we are meant to guide each other. Freedom is always available when we soften into it.

Stay Present No Matter What

From an energy perspective, you invite in negativity when you're not present. Have you ever had one of those days where you tripped and hurt yourself, spilled your coffee, and missed your exit all in quick succession? "Where am I?" you might ask after all that, because you're definitely not here and now! Spacing out like this tends to downward spiral until you catch it and change it.

I believe that pain increases the likelihood we'll disconnect. Of course, there is the physical pain of illness or injury. We check out when we're tired. And we also don't want to feel everything when someone reminds us of a difficult parent or past partner, or of the time we got bullied or rejected. These less-tangible forms of pain simmer beneath the surface of our consciousness, as we go float on the ceiling until that trigger goes away.

In addition, it may be hard to stay present when you're bored. When you want things to be different than they are, if you're feeling stuck behind the picket fence or inside the cubicle—you zone out. With that relationship that's grown too predictable, when you don't feel aligned, or where you believe someone's not at your level, are you able to be grounded and connected? Should you be?

In the past, I went to many seminars as a white belt. While most of my training partners were engaged and welcoming, I met a handful of people who attacked halfway, threw me hesitantly, and looked around the room as we practiced. Of course, some may have had their personal reasons for being distracted, which had nothing to do with me. In other cases, I imagine they dismissed me due to my belt color, and assumed I needed coddling. Given my dedication to Aikido, I felt unmet. Weren't these folks supposed to be an example for me to follow? I didn't want to.

That said, I can relate to wanting to train fast and hard. I, too, have been frustrated and antsy when running through the same basic moves, over and over. I have struggled to stay open when a teacher talked longer than I wanted to listen. "Just take it in," I told myself at one weekend seminar. "You can go back to your normal training on Monday."

I do my best now to find patience and generosity with newer students, with senpai who talk down to me, or with teachers with whom I don't resonate. Even if I'm bored with the technique or training style, I can take interest and see what I discover. I don't know what I don't know. There is always something to learn or experience. And, Aikido would blend with all these things, not just with the young whippersnappers that hover at the sensei's feet and throw each other around like rag dolls. For Aikido to carry forth, we need to meet everyone who sincerely walks through the door, right where they are.

While we can and should choose our teachers, jobs, friends, and life partners—we don't get everything we want, even in the best of cases. Many wonder how much to compromise and how much to go their own way. When we compromise from a place of frustration, from a place of *can't have it all*, we end up repressing life force. No wonder we don't want to do it! Living that way too long can shave years off of our lives.

If the idea of compromise evokes this fear of soul-death, what if we come to acceptance? Since acceptance stems from the consciousness of "I can include this" when living with something we don't prefer, we open here rather than contract. Boundaries are still fine and good, and some things are not up for negotiation. Yet when we willingly choose to compromise with full acceptance, compromise will cease. If we're going to do something, we may as well do it all the way.

The paradox here is that as soon as we accept something fully, we see solutions that we couldn't see when we were triggered, defending our needs at all costs. New possibilities may appear, seemingly out of nowhere. Or we may realize a blessing in disguise embedded in apparently fateful reality.

It's not nicer to divide ourselves because we don't want to be where we're at. This is not Aikido. This is not the art of love. When we do it, we lose integrity and, in a sense, we live as empty shells. We dishonor our own life and everyone around us. Just as we must cut decisively when wielding a sword, it's better to be clear about one choice or another than to fumble around. If your truth is *I don't know*, you can still sit still in that truth versus ping-ponging between unreal maybes.

We should stop convincing ourselves that going numb will protect us. Of course, many of these coping mechanisms began in childhood and are running unconsciously in the background. I love Aikido because it actually requires full presence! Knowing I'll risk injury if I check out, I stay in my body. I can't think about what happened earlier or what's going on later. If I was preoccupied with something before class, I'm rarely worried about it when I leave. Clicking into fully being here now is one of the most energizing, healing, and protective choices we can make.

If They Flicker, Let Your Light Overflow

Hopefully, you find a partner in life who can meet you fully. In other relationships—whether they be personal, business, or on the Aikido mat—you'll inevitably be called to show up at your best with *all* types of people. This can be a challenge.

It's one thing to be patient with the ignorant, or to peacefully retain your dignity with those who are rude or arrogant. What if someone just doesn't have the capacity to meet you in reciprocity? Is there a way to help the other person without compromising yourself? Is it possible to stay engaged and live as your amazing self, even when they're not giving you much?

When this happens for me during Aikido training, it helps me to recall the exhilaration of training with someone who brings a lot of energy. I remember how electric it was when we came together. And then no matter how my next partner shows up, I can click back into that feeling and allow it to overflow from within me. In this case, I am neither giving myself away nor repressing my spirit entirely. I am having and sharing. From this stance, I am also fine to tone it down. Because as long as I feel full and fluid, I am operating from discernment rather than repression.

The more you put into something, the more you typically get back. The key is to give from that wellspring within you, versus overreaching to achieve an external result. If you come on strong, either with a training partner or with someone in your life, you'd better be prepared to handle their response.

Firing away without thinking, you're more likely to get hurt. Responding from your center with the same excitement, both you and your partner get to enjoy a powerful dance of energies. Rather than *giving it your all* all the time, I suggest *being* your all, all the time. And your "all" will include slowing down when either you or your partner need to. It may require a pause or redirect that you didn't want or plan on. Your "all" won't mind, and everyone will keep having a good time.

Only Run If You're Being Chased

In my kids' classes, we play a lot of tag games. I sometimes stop and ask, "Who has a strategy to share? If you're good at tag, what's your secret?" At this prompt, they'll shout out many secrets, but I rarely hear mine.

My best tip to anyone playing tag is this: Only run if you're being chased. Over and over, I see kids running madly around the whole time. Sure, they may have tons of energy to burn! But if they would only notice that the person who's *it* is nowhere near them, they could catch a breather. In conserving energy this way, they'd easily sprint, and escape being tagged when needed.

I talked earlier about the power and mastery in purposeful non-action. This definitely has a place. More frequently, we'll be faced with situations that require appropriate, timely, measured action. This is about putting the right amount of energy into something.

When you don't give enough energy, your partner can't practice. Your lover gets hurt or mad. Your boss gives you notice. Your kid gets in trouble or feels forlorn. As long as you pay attention and stay centered, these situations are rare. If they still occur, because you don't have the skill or confidence to offer the energy a situation warrants, there is still a remedy: own what's happening. If you ask for help versus clamping down, you'll move in the right direction.

Conversely, over-functioning can exhaust you. Unknowingly, you could push people away, even if you intend the opposite. At best, they scratch their heads, wondering why you're doing this. In more severe cases, some folks feel penned in or fight back. Hyperdrive is rarely a setting that supports love.

Both running mindlessly and freezing come from the same guarded, fearful place within you. On each side of the coin, you don't allow connection and so you cannot feel for what's appropriate. You force out the joy, success, and potential you deep down long for. Attempting to outsmart any possible hurt, you actually make yourself more vulnerable.

Using the right amount of energy at all times requires subtle skill and continual practice. It's never the same from person to person, instance to instance. You probably have at least one person in your world who's readily triggered, and another with thicker skin. The gentle approach that evokes positive change in the sensitive soul would not be enough to get the hardier one's attention. And if you were equally as blunt with your delicate friend as you were with the other, you'd risk overwhelming them.

Personality types are one factor. Also to consider are the conditions of the moment. Are you over-communicating and anxiously chasing your partner when she's already inundated with work? Did she sleep last night? Are you catching her starving, or on the way to meet her most difficult family member?

Withholding can also backfire. Have you ever waited so long to communicate, that you're all pent up inside about a certain relationship? Maybe it's been weeks since you've heard from your new love interest or job prospect, and you're uncomfortable because you thought things were going somewhere. Or perhaps you're looking for those always elusive, perfect conditions to share your heart. In this case, stop. You owe it to yourself to reach out. It's not about whose turn it is or whose job it is at this point. You are not giving enough energy to support the flow or love and life here.

Do your part to keep things moving, *as life dictates*. That may require pausing when there's no value in acting, so that you have capacity to do so when the time comes. And sometimes it means: Get off your butt! There is always the chance of a disappointing outcome, however as long as you're in your heart and truth, that's better than a stalemate. We can always regroup and forge onward, as long as we un-stop the kinks where energy wants to flow. It is a law of physics that energy cannot be created or destroyed, but it can be changed from one form to another. To this end, it can be saved and skillfully rationed. No matter what, the only way to win is to work with it.

Don't Want It, Create It

I have taught quite a few manifesting workshops, using guided meditation and other creative practices. In these workshops, I'll ask participants to release all the *wanting* energy around their goals. While positive emotions do assist us in realizing our dreams, wanting is a slippery slope.

Wanting implies not having. If you had, you wouldn't want! It actually repels the thing you want, because your frequency doesn't match how it feels to have it.

Think about one thing that's easy in your life, for which you are super grateful. Maybe it's your home, your job, your partner, your health, your finances, great friends, or something else. Most of us obsess about our challenges and take the easy things for granted. Whatever your easy area is, you probably don't think much about it. It's just a given. And here, there is no wanting. I wonder what life would be like, if we transferred this same feeling to our still unmet desires? As hard as this may seem, it may be worth it to fake it till you make it.

Recently, I made a request of someone, about something dear to me. I'd made similar requests before and hadn't gotten what I wanted. On the advice of a friend, I phrased my latest message like this, "Hey, I want to let you know what I'm envisioning ... Does this work for you?" And, he said yes!

Looking back at my prior text to him about this same subject, I'd been less certain. The request seemed complicated and if I were him, I might not have taken it seriously or agreed to it. I realized that back then, I did not believe I would get what I was asking for. I wanted it but wasn't *having* it. No wonder it hadn't happened.

In Aikido training, flow goes out the window as soon as we want a certain outcome. I'm guilty of this as much as anyone. Let's say I get a bright idea during freestyle practice. I want to do something fancy, and I get my head around it—only to find that it's not there when uke attacks. From this mindset, the interaction almost always goes south. What I wanted to do doesn't work, but I've already invested my energy into that idea. In most cases, this makes it too late to switch to a more appropriate response in time.

That said, we can often command our partners' movements, assuming we're sure of ourselves. If they are able to do a breakfall, we can require it of them. However, as soon as we want to show off by making them breakfall, it's less potent and less safe. Feeling the truth of the moment, this works when we move from knowing the next movement is already there. On some level, it is.

Years ago, my friend got a new job, and it felt really good to her. I asked her how she manifested it, and she said, "I just knew it was going to happen, and I didn't worry about it." I loved that reminder and have found it true. She is still at that job seven years later. When something is aligned, effort is not needed. Effort can actually mess it up.

The certainty that comes with creating intentionally is a relaxed power. It works because it's both responsive and proactive. It's about dancing with Universal forces. And when we do, things are simple and clear.

Writing Practice:
Moving from Wanting to Having

1. Which aspects of your life or relationships are easy for you?

2. What are your beliefs and assumptions about these things?

3. Name some things you'd like to improve in your relationships, particularly if you've been feeling stuck or ineffective in making changes.

4. How can you shift your beliefs about the hard things? What would it look like to apply your beliefs about the easy things to these challenges? Describe how you might move from wanting to having it.

Focus Forward

"But Lot's wife looked back, and she became a pillar of salt" (*The Bible*, Genesis 19.26).

"Don't look back" is a common saying, and the verse above illustrates the potential danger in doing so. This aligns with Aikido wisdom, where a forward mindset proves essential for safety and connection.

There is a saying in our practice: "Push, don't pull." Each movement you make should be a courageous choice. Even when apparently moving backwards, your focus should be forward. Your hips, gaze, and hands all demonstrate this. We step back merely to better our position, not to retreat.

From a martial standpoint, you leave yourself vulnerable to attack or injury when you look back. Your interaction with your partner is not in the past, it's only in the now. You are most protected when you show up for what's presently happening, as you simultaneously anticipate what's next. The goal is to intercept the next blow before it happens, or to anchor the outcome you desire by being ahead of it. To be effective, you must do this while remaining centered. This will make your next move that much stronger, and you'll also be ready in case conditions change.

With the goal of conscious union, it's confounding to your partner when you say, "Hey, let's go here," as you simultaneously look backwards. In this case, why should they follow you? You don't appear to mean what you say. By contrast, when your actions are consistent, you become trustable. Then, you lead without trying.

Sometimes, looking back shows up in obvious ways, such as ruminating about the past, grieving a loss, or comparing a current lover to a former one. There can be value in this type of reflection in appropriate proportion, while also tending to the bigger picture of life unfolding.

The more insidious ways we focus backwards include complaining, judging, and repeating stories of what's not working. "I don't want any more XYZ" tends to reinforce XYZ, for instance, whereas requesting what you *do* want makes it easier to get it.

We also baffle our loved ones when we react to current situations with unintegrated emotions from the past. Maybe your lover did something you didn't like, and then you exploded, way out of proportion to the situation. This is an after-effect of having previously checked out, repressed your feelings, or withheld your truth—perhaps even with a different person. Those emotions must come out at some point, and at that point they seem to have no context.

Particularly when it comes to early childhood patterning, we don't always realize our tendencies until they get in our way enough times as adults. While healing can take some time and often professional support, Aikido is a great way to retrain us without necessarily digging into the *why* of what we do.

On the mat, if you keep pulling away from your partner and then realize that connection stops every time you do, you'll change that habit pretty quick. If you get hit because you pause too long wondering how to move, you'll see how moving may be safer than thinking. Because we don't stop to talk things through in Aikido practice, we limit the tendency to overanalyze. Either your interaction with partner clicks or it doesn't, and it's pretty obvious if you just keep training. Inevitably, healthier patterns become natural.

This forward focus is also a giving mindset. We give by sharing energy or offering direction. We take by whining, withholding, or constant rewinding. Whether on the mat or in life, your partner has already offered their precious time and energy to be with you. How can you join them in a life-giving way?

Step Back to Get Leverage

When you hit a wall in conversation with a loved one, if you're too fried to get any more work done, or when you're fighting an illness—you rest. If you've been reaching out to that special someone without them initiating as much in return, you might pull back. These instincts are natural. We are all seeking balance and self-protection.

Though we keep a forward focus in Aikido, there are times when a strategic step back is the best way to move things along. If your uke has your wrist and you increase the space between you and her, she stretches to keep holding on and so loses her balance. You just took her down with little effort. With your bokken (practice sword), you might realize that you're too close to cut your partner's wrist. You can adjust your stance, still facing your partner as you step back to a more effective position. These movements are not from fear; far from it.

Knowing when and how to step back requires acute spatial awareness, and full attunement with your environment. Newer students may try harder by getting closer, only to find themselves butting into their partners' strength.

Of course, a step back is also needed when you are in danger. For example, in working too hard to affect your partner, you might put yourself in a compromised position. Finding yourself inches from your partner's fist, that's a good time to step back!

In personal relationships, we chance pushing someone away when we don't give them enough space. If we can trade this nervous fear for trust, it's easy to see what to do. Yet when we push forward and stop doing our own self-care in order to please another, our efforts are futile. We show up with a shorter fuse. It's hard to pull love from another when we're not loving ourselves first.

Consciously drawing your energy in at select times actually *feeds* the relational harmony, even when outward appearances or habitual programming indicate differently. The truth is: quiet mastery goes further than effort.

Mindfully stepping back takes practice. It may be uncomfortable, and your loved ones might get fussy as you find your way. The more poised and filled with love you are, the quicker everyone's tension will dissipate. Reminder: Being filled with love implies self-love as your baseline. In these moments, you step back from a *yes* consciousness. It is a *yes* to yourself, and to the whole of the interaction.

People can feel the difference when you move from *yes* versus *no*, or from love versus fear. And this is where we turn backwards yet continue to face forward.

Honor Where You Came From

Stepping backwards in the larger sense means honoring where we've come from. I haven't always understood this, yet I have come to appreciate it. It is implicit in Aikido, and it helps us live and love as integrated beings.

I have always been a willful one, due both to my soul's truth as well as a childhood coping strategy. In the process of deepening my own training and eventually stepping into the role of Aikido teacher and dojo owner, I started to see the value of lineage. I realized I was not simply a business owner or instructor, but more importantly, a lineage keeper. I hold this as a deep honor and responsibility.

Since the late 1990s I have known many teachers, including master teachers—of both Aikido and other spiritual traditions. Just like parents and others we're told to look up to, it's disappointing to see when a teacher is driven by ego. We are all human, and these impulses show up to some degree in most of us. They express in different ways—such as competing rather than cooperating, needing adoration from followers, needing impressive followers, or conversely not being willing to support those coming up.

Many of us have baggage around not being led or cared for the way we needed by our elders. This can make us hyper-individualistic, and suspicious of all guidance. We might feel that respecting those who went before us is anything from irrelevant to uncool to dangerous. I get it. We may have been asked to respect people who weren't worthy of that respect.

What can result here, though, are unhealthy habits that perpetuate more of what we don't want. These habits include attachment to being right, rigidity, and holding the world on our shoulders. These things stunt our growth and sabotage our relationships.

We don't always have to look up the totem pole for guidance. It's sometimes a lover or friend who mirrors something valuable back to us. But rebelling against those who we perceive to be above us can put us in a guarded state with everybody. It can cloud all our mirrors, to the point we cannot see ourselves. We are not always fully self-aware and so sometimes, we should trust our partners more than we trust ourselves. This works when you have a conscious, loving relationship which is relatively free of ego. It also works in Aikido training when we each commit to support community, within the container of the dojo and with good leadership.

In larger society, we're seeing a movement towards individualism, anything goes, and creative freedom. There's a trend away from hierarchical power structures, and to an extent I align with this. I value sovereignty. I believe we each have direct access to God or the Divine, and that this is healthy and empowering.

Our Aikido etiquette has shown me a beautiful balance in this regard. We have hierarchical roles based in rank and experience, and yet everyone is worthy of equal respect. Some may wonder how both can be true.

In all the current talk of equality, I think there is a dangerous tendency to think everyone is the same. We're not. Equality does not equal sameness. We can have equal value, but different roles and gifts.

For instance, I have very little interest or knowledge in mechanics. It would be ridiculous for me to try to fix my own car. On the other side, there are things I am highly experienced at, and it would be a disservice for me to not offer these gifts to the world. Each of us receives more value out of life when we accept and honor our Divine path, and that of one another.

Equality in a marriage may look like one stay-at-home-parent and one breadwinner. It might express as one scattered yet expansive thinker and another introverted planner and grounding force. It could be that one person is really spiritual and the other is highly logical. We don't have to split the rent, chores, and all the skills 50/50. Hopefully, we appreciate one another and ourselves enough to shine as we are and let others do the same. Ideally, we see how the whole is greater than the sum of its parts when we join forces.

Some of us need to step up and share ourselves more boldly, without reservation. And for the strong and successful types, we must learn to let go and receive more.

Even if no one in our past guided us well, that doesn't mean all input is bad. As a student, I look for healthy role models because I know I need them for my own evolution. As a parent, I'm committed to giving my daughter what I did not receive growing up. Having learned from experience, I do my best to serve anytime I'm in a leadership role. And I invest when I find trustworthy guidance.

I have come to see receiving as an act of self-worth. Low self-worth will enforce the perception that no one can assist or inspire you. This is a lie. If your Aikido practice, your life path, or your relationships are important to you, seek supportive mentorship. This is an honoring, both of yourself and those you influence. It is neither selfish nor unsafe, when seen through this lens.

Receiving doesn't make us weak; it is how we become great. It is a gift to those who give to us. Aikido in particular is an energy exchange, which comes alive in relationship. It is not simply a physical practice. You can obsess over getting things "right" on the mat, at work, or in your love life. But no one cares about how perfect you are in isolation.

Do we all want to copy our parents' marriages or life conditions? Probably not. Should we become cookie-cutter copies of our teachers? I don't think a good teacher would want that. And yet, releasing any charge around where we came from is necessary to go where we're going. Not receiving what we want or need provides clarity for what we value. Living into this value leads to success.

Show Don't Tell

In Aikido, more experienced students are supposed to model sincere, correct practice to the best of their ability. The tradition is largely "show, don't tell," without talking unless necessary. Often warm-ups and demonstrations are conducted in complete silence, requiring us to pay close attention and get out of our heads. I love this and find it therapeutic, though it takes getting used to for many.

In your relationships, do you remember a time when someone said one thing and did another? Have you ever gotten lost in someone's words? Do you sometimes not know what to say? Words are not necessarily trustworthy, nor are they always forthcoming. Bodies don't lie, and we must look at what people actually do. Obviously as a writer I love words, yet words may be overrated.

Right after college, I spent seven weeks at a yoga ashram in the redwoods near Santa Cruz, California. The guru there was silent, and he communicated by writing on a handheld chalkboard when he needed to. With the support of this community, I decided to go silent for two weeks. I was astounded at how much my life force increased, and at how little I even needed to use my chalkboard. So much was conveyed through energy and body language! I wonder if I'd previously been leaking energy, through unintegrated communication.

Various spiritual traditions believe that the vibration of words and sounds have mystical powers. If this is true, perhaps we should not abandon words, but instead be sure we use them wisely.

Strong beginners in Aikido are not only the most dangerous physically; they are also more likely to talk through practice. With anything that takes a long time to learn, it's exciting to feel like we are getting somewhere. Once we know a lot more than we used to, we want to share! This is true in playing an instrument, in cultivating a new relationship, or pursuing a new job or business. The paradox is that as soon as we believe we know something or someone, our connection stagnates. In each of these cases, there is still so much we don't know. Curiosity and humility will keep love and learning alive, each step of the way.

Certain personality types like to talk and have answers from the get-go, as well as after decades of experience. Some folks learn best through verbal cues, and others need words of affirmation or for information. More commonly, the most masterful Aikido partners are the quietest.

Have you ever met someone who was so grounded and self-assured, they didn't need to flaunt it? One example is the wealthy person who drives a beat-up car. By contrast, some narcissistic types communicate in "word salad." This means they talk on and on and on yet leave you wondering what they just said. Their words don't necessarily make sense. It's quite exhausting to be on the receiving end of this.

I tell my students, "If you know it, show it." While I have done my share of talking though techniques, I see now how talking is not always optimal. If you've previously gotten validation for your intelligence, it's tempting. It takes maturity to allow your actions to speak for themselves, and to let others be.

Let's say there's someone you really care about. How could you show them versus telling them? What would it take to build trust with your employer or client? Or with a new acquaintance, are they giving you reason to trust or are they just telling you to? Here, time illuminates the truth.

Curtailing the impulse to speak reveals what's real. For someone dishonest—even if they're mainly dishonest with themselves—this is hard to do. Silence cuts through both illusion and delusion.

Too much talking can also preclude your partner from finding their own breakthrough. I am more of a *feeler* than a *talker*, and I learn by doing. I've had many experiences of short-circuiting because my Aikido partner talked faster than I could feel. I've experienced a similar shutdown when someone pattered on and on about a subject they knew well, but that I didn't. I needed them to slow down so I could ask questions, try out the concepts, and make sure I understood. Because of this, I try not to talk over someone else's process.

I am careful with my words in daily life. Words have creative power. Just as a small child could throw a 6'-tall man by using her ki and proper position, a few words can make a huge impact when they align with the speaker's thoughts, feelings, and physical reality. Considering that love and harmony are based in unity, misaligned words muck things up. Most of us could talk less and reflect more before sharing.

The power of words weaves through many spiritual traditions. It is known by many wise souls. And words that don't match reality are said to cause chaos and destruction.

How to Handle Overwhelm

Modern life has ceaseless demands. Juggling work, family, love, self-care, home life, friends, hobbies, and all of our tasks can be overwhelming. Now, we have the increased pull of technology, which can be hard to shut off. It's easy to feel that life is happening *to* us, and that we're putting out fires all the time. Because of this, we could all learn to master ourselves in the face of overwhelm.

Proactive confidence is keenly illustrated in Aikido randori, the practice of defending oneself against multiple opponents. If you just wait and see what happens when five people surround you, you're toast. The way to succeed here is to take charge from the outset, moving towards person after person as you invite them to attack. Based on how you place yourself, you not only motivate your ukes to strike in certain ways, but you also throw them towards the people most likely to attack next, buying yourself time.

Surprisingly, your smooth, controlled pace will slow the momentum of those coming at you. By contrast, your jumpy nervousness tends to bring spastic, unwelcome fire from your adversaries. This is equally true in 1/1 training and in all of life, where what we put out dictates what we get. Yet it's especially impressive in randori—maybe because it triggers an intimidating mob mentality.

Life can feel like randori these days. Many of us say, "When does it ever stop? What should I pay attention to next? I'm being pulled in so many directions I can't even think straight. Days go by and I don't do the thing I value most."

Besides having too much on your plate, overwhelm can occur when intimacy surpasses what you're used to, or when you push past your familiar patterns. This can happen with health goals, at work, or with friends and family—not just with romantic love. But I would argue that overwhelm is more systemic and less specific. We feel it when we don't have enough space (whether that be physical space or a spacious perspective), and when we don't stand in confidence.

When we sit in the driver's seat of our own life and live intentionally, open to possibility, nothing is too big to handle. If we allow ourselves to get frazzled by every bid for our attention, and dazzled by every bright, shiny, object, it's all too much. One text message may as well be five 300-pound guys if you're off-balance to begin with. Those same guys are nothing if you stay calm and circle them, instead of letting them surround you.

These times can be dizzying, but we have a choice. The good news is: With the world at our fingertips, we each have a multitude of opportunity to love and connect. How can you choose your connections more consciously? Can you imagine being the director of your attention? What might it look like to stay empowered as you do?

Stay In Control

A successful company succeeds in part because it has policies. Within the bounds of these rules, the business flourishes. While they're less likely to be in writing, a marriage may have similar agreements. This creates assurance for the partners. Because they aren't wondering what's expected all the time, love can grow fuller and deeper.

In parenting or teaching small children, boundaries are essential. These young beings are new to the 3-D world, which is why they seem so magical. Yet, they need help to navigate how to live in their bodies, in a world with limits, and in relationship to other people. Caregivers who match the children's unbound spirits all the time fail to provide this. They may hold back in offering discipline, for fear of being mean or unpopular. Yet, there are ways to kindly, clearly show a child the rules. When the child acts out or pushes boundaries, they are looking for clarity and guidance. They are not always seeking freedom, nor are they necessarily indicating that the caregiver's rules are inappropriate. Of course, we should not be too harsh or disrespectful.

Like any sport with the potential for injury, Aikido requires we stay in control. As much as we can accelerate or increase power, we should equally be able to stop as needed. This includes stopping our partner's momentum as well as our own. When you're in the guiding role, a skilled partner will follow you. They will spin if you keep spinning, and they'll settle if you bring them to a halt. There is that saying, "with great power comes great responsibility."

When a partner or love interest feels our composure, they trust us more. Conversely, always pressing for *harder, faster, more* is suspect. It feels unsafe. As fun as it may be for a bit, we know it's not sustainable and so we withhold—even a little part of ourselves. Paradoxically, we love more fully when we know there are boundaries. We jump in the river when we see the bank.

At the beginning in learning Aikido, in getting to know a new person, or in pursuing a new endeavor, we want to stay safe while we get our bearings. As we build momentum and start to hit the gas, control seems to go out the window. It should still be there in our toolbox. Knowing we can hit the brakes at any time gives a boost to our power. This type of control does not squelch life force. It cherishes it. It protects by being there when needed, and it respects by allowing loving energy to flow abundantly.

Finish Strong

How you end one thing determines how you begin the next thing. When it comes time to end anything—be it a relationship, a day, a project, or phase of life—are you conscious, or are you distracted and rushing off?

I talked earlier about the importance of proper foundation, and how the quality of any beginning determines what will follow. It is all a circle. Beginnings ultimately lead to endings. Endings become beginnings before you can blink. There is no insignificant moment in conscious relationship, or in a conscious life.

Most of us are not used to sustaining this level of presence. Aikido beginners and children, especially, will throw their partner and then fidget, fix their hair, or take a bunch of extra steps. Are they releasing the tension around getting it right? Possibly. Are they unaccustomed to the intimacy? Maybe. Is it intentional? Unlikely. Is it martial? Definitely not.

And I believe their partner could feel that they were less than all there. You cannot execute an integrated act and end up scattered. Your true power will show in your finish.

In Aikido we have a term for this: *zanshin*. It refers to being settled after a throw, but also to having vast and continuous awareness. Zanshin includes good posture, finishing in *kamai* (ready stance), and facing your partner. Maybe he'll come back your way and maybe he won't, but this ending respects you both.

Every relationship you have comes down to you. If you go through a loving divorce, you'll bring that love into any new relationships. When you feel complete with your last job, knowing you'd done everything you could to tie up loose ends and communicate as needed, you'll feel so free and worthy entering your next venture. Having the chance to resolve your issues with a family member before they pass gives you both greater peace, gratitude, and volition to move forward—however that looks.

Endings tend to get bypassed in our culture, and so we suffer a lot. Death, divorce, plans that don't pan out, or losses are seen as negative. This is neither necessary nor helpful. Every beginning requires an ending, and so make your endings good. Being fully present for love means all of you shows up for all of that. And then you'll be the first to spot the sun peeking up over the horizon.

Glossary

Aikido- the way of harmonizing with life force

Aikidoka- one who practices Aikido

Atemi- a strike or pose done to distract or disrupt partner as you apply technique

Budo- the martial way, the way of the warrior (which includes purification of mind, body, and spirit)

Dojo- the place where Aikido is practiced

Domo arigato gozaimashita- thank you very much

Gi- also known as do-gi, an Aikido uniform

Hanmi- "half body"—basic triangular Aikido stance, with one foot in front

Henka waza- changing from one technique to another

Irimi- entering movement, typically stepping forward with the back foot

Jiyu waza- freestyle practice

Kaeshi waza- reversing technique, where uke becomes nage and vice versa

Kamai- "ready" position, in hanmi with hands in front

Ki- energy, life force

Kihon waza- fundamental technique

Kokyu dosa- seated breath throw

Kuzushi- breaking balance

Maai- appropriate spacing, distance of engagement between partners

Musubi- connection

Nage- the one who is attacked and then executes technique

Nikkyo- second technique, incorporating a wrist lock

Onegaishimasu- please will you practice with me?

Randori- defending oneself against multiple attackers

Senpai- a practitioner ranked higher than you, or who attained the same rank at an earlier date

Sensei- teacher

Tenkan- turning movement, done by pivoting and stepping back

Tenshin- stepping back and changing hanmi

Uke- one who attacks and then must respond to partner's technique

Ukemi- the art of receiving, including but not limited to falls and rolls

Waza- technique

Zanshin- continual awareness, mindfulness from start to finish

Acknowledgments

I have had a lot of obvious support along my journey that led to this book, and some less obvious support. I'll start with the obvious.

Thank you to all my Aikido teachers, beginning in 1996 with Jude Blitz Sensei and then Hiroshi Ikeda Shihan, Tres Hofmeister Sensei, and everyone at Boulder Aikikai. To Lee Lavi Ramirez Sensei who welcomed both my daughter and I for a brief stint at North Valley Aikikai in Los Angeles. To Mike Jones, who strongly influenced both my technique and teaching style, and who introduced me to the United States Aikido Federation (USAF). To Chris Bergerud and to everyone at Roaring Fork Aikikai, my home away from home for three years. To Reuven Lirov Sensei for your trust in sponsoring me when I found myself without dojo or teacher. To everyone at Pinellas County Aikikai and Florida Aikikai, especially Peter Bernath Shihan and Penny Bernath Shihan.

As an intuitive, I wonder if my instructor thought I was crazy years ago when I mentioned feeling the presence of certain Aikido teachers who had passed. Most notably, I have felt guided by the spirits of Morihei Ueshiba (aka O Sensei), the founder of Aikido, and Seiichi Sugano Shihan. I give thanks to each of these teachers, though we never met in the 3-D.

To the USAF and to all who keep it running, especially Laura Jacobs Pavlick Shihan and Karen De Paola Shihan, thank you. You help ensure the integrity of our Aikido, and you support our dojos and community.

Often, others sense your destiny even when you do not. Thank you to Burt Oglesby for the gift of your handmade kamiza and weapons after you retired from teaching. When I said, "I don't know if I'll ever use these. Are you sure you want to give them to me?" you looked me straight in the eye and said, "Yes." To Carolyn Oswald and your family, for the gift of weapons and gis as I was starting my Aikido program.

Aikido is like an extended family, and this wouldn't be complete without thanking my Aikido friends. Cristina Costanzo, I appreciate all your encouragement, especially your nudge to find the right direction when I did not know how to proceed, and for your feedback on this book in process. Helen Reynolds, thank you for your astute insights on this manuscript, not to mention your support of my daughter and her training. Matt Addison, thank you for coming out to Colorado and down to Ft. Lauderdale as I was prepping for testing. To all my community and training partners, I give thanks for all I have learned from you and for the bond we share beyond words.

In 2022, I walked into the HeartBarn at 13 Moons Ranch in Carbondale, Colorado. Sitting on beautiful land right on the Crystal River at the base of Mt. Sopris, it was still partially under construction. Yet, in the pregnant pause of not seeing if or how my Aikido would re-emerge, in the openness of *nothing* that became *something*, a knowing came through me as if from above. I looked at the martial arts mats on the floor, and heard, "It's time to start teaching Aikido again, and this is your space." And three years later, at the time of this writing, Crystal River Aikikai is running strong out of the HeartBarn. Infinite gratitude to Oriana Moebius, to your family, and to everyone who has helped to manage this space.

I am super grateful for all my Aikido students, and to

their families who support them. My students' progress and dedication help the art to continue. By teaching, I've had the opportunity to polish my technique, to become really clear, and to find Aikido with all types of people who are not trained to play along.

Beyond Aikido, I give thanks to all the clients to whom I have counseled and offered healing sessions. I learn so much from each of you! And while I am known as a seer, being able to see things in other people has illuminated so many relational dynamics that are hard to spot without re-al-life examples.

Each of my partners on and off the mat, and through all types of relationships, has made their way into this book somewhere. Thank you for sharing your energy with me.

It takes a team to publish a book. I appreciate Susan Mitchell for your keen editing and Alyssa Ohnmacht for layout. Thank you to Lucinda Raye for your brilliant cover art and web design. Mike Beas, thank you once again for your marketing wizardry. To Elysia Skye for narration and to Zach Kasik at Wild Feather Recording for the audio book production, I am grateful. And Zita Xavier, your feedback was the perfect redirect when I hit a stuck point midway through writing.

I also give thanks for some less obvious blessings in disguise:

Just as unity on the mat is that much more meaningful in the face of conflict, I recognize the *No's* I got that spiraled me into Divine alignment and fueled my deeper *Yes's*. When the world shut down for "two weeks to slow the curve" and then our former dojo shut down for 15 months, where it barely reopened and then closed permanently, when my teacher quit—in each of these cases I had to do henka waza. I needed to change course. Particularly with the forced break, I had to be ok with not knowing, with trusting the process. I had no guarantees if or how I'd get back to Aikido. I had to respond appropriately each step of the way, all the while not giving up.

Not having a local teacher or school already set up, I was blessed to step into leadership and service. Having been an entrepreneur and teacher my whole adult life, this feels joyful to my creative spirit. I have the energy and dedication, and I believe that because of this, the way has been offered me.

May I continue to utilize and share what I've been given and continue to receive, in the most life-giving ways for all concerned. Domo arigato gozaimashita.

About the Author

Ann O'Brien is an Aikido teacher and spiritual guide. She began both her Aikido and intuitive training in the 1990's, and went on to study yoga, holistic health and conscious relationships. Since 2004, she has supported clients with 1/1 coaching and energy healing as well as classes in intuitive and personal development. Ann is also the author of two #1 Amazon best-sellers, *A Woman's Guide to Conscious Love* and *Everyone Is Psychic*.

Learn more at www.AnnOBrienLiving.com
or scan this QR code:

www.ingramcontent.com/pod-product-compliance
Lightning Source LLC
Chambersburg PA
CBHW031124020426
42333CB00012B/217